A VIRGINIAN IN BEST BLUE

First published in 2004 by

WOODFIELD PUBLISHING
Bognor Regis, West Sussex, England
www.woodfieldpublishing.com

© Parke F Smith, 2004

ISBN 1-903953-61-8

A Virginian in Best Blue

A US Pilot's Experiences in the
Royal Air Force 1942-46

PARKE F. SMITH

Woodfield

The Bells of Hell go ting-a-ling-a-ling, for you but not for me...

Dedicated to the memory of friends and fellow pilots who unselfishly paid the ultimate price:

Unattached RAF, 1942 to 1943	
P/O Elliot, Java	P/O Hawley, S. America
Lt Huntsinger, Calif USA	Lt Koons, Montana USA
Lt Murray, Mass USA	
No. 253 Squadron RAF, August to December 1943	
F/O Adams, Canada	P/O McKay, Canada
No. 225 Squadron RAF, December 1943 to May 1944	
P/O Milton, Russo-UK	Sgt Dear, Australia
F/O McDonald, UK	P/O Leith-Hay-Clark, UK
P/O Cable, UK	P/O Finney, Canada
Lt Theobald, S. Africa	F/O Smart, UK
Sgt Melville, UK	Lt Brandie, S. Africa
P/O McCall, UK	F/O Walton, UK
F/O McCloud, Scotland	Lt Thompson, S. Africa
Sgt Wooten, UK	Sgt Whittaker, UK
Lt Arryonson, S. Africa	P/O Pratt, UK
No. 65 Squadron RAF, March to April 1945	
S/Ldr Hill, UK	F/Lt Bradford, UK
F/Lt Whatt, UK	F/Lt Butler, UK
S/Ldr Stewart, UK	F/Lt Young, UK
No. 41 Operational Training Unit RAF	
P/O Varley, UK (1942)	F/Lt Cauldwell, Canada (1945)
US Naval Air Service, November 1943	
Lt James A. Smith III, Virginia USA (Author's brother)	

The Author, Capodicino, Italy 1943.

For Alice and our children,
Christie, James, Preston & Parke

My theatre of operations 1941-46.

Contents

Foreword – by Alex Henshaw MBE

How much better history would be served if all the disastrous upheavals that have made such a great impact on our civilization could have been described and recorded at the time by the participants?

Historical researchers into our past often do an excellent job, and few would quarrel with their facts. As good as this may be, however, they can never unveil the anguish, the pain, the courage and the fortitude of those men and women, who through no fault of their own, were caught up in a maelstrom from which there was no escape.

To me, as an Englishman, Parke's memoirs come across as the personal recollections of a full-blooded, young American who left a happy and well established home in Virginia; he was driven by deep-founded convictions to fight for a foreign power at a time of isolationist policies within his own government, and for a cause in which so many had made the ultimate sacrifice.

His narrative is composed in a readable, straightforward manner without undue embellishment; in the way a father would tell his family the honest story of dramatic events into which he was drawn in his own youth – events which undoubtedly influenced the development of his own maturity.

As Chief Test Pilot for Vickers-Supermarine, manufacturers of the Spitfire, I was briefed to visit No. 41 Operational Training

Unit at Hawarden to demonstrate the better qualities of the machine before a group of young RAF officers being prepared for battle. Parke, already in the RAF at that time and being a witness, wrote some forty years later, reminding me of the occasion. Since that somewhat hurried and impersonal visit to Hawarden it has been my privilege to meet and enjoy a friendship with Parke and his charming wife Alice that I value most highly.

For those like myself who remember the Great War of 1917-18, Parke's World War II memoirs bring back those almost forgotten mental pictures of traumatic events in a child's mind that can never really be erased. Particularly, the heart-rending sobs of my mother, grandmother and aunt when they saw the morning paper with the rows and rows of casualties covering so many pages after the battle of the Somme. Then there was the joy and relief as we later watched those fine, energetic young men from the USA who arrived to help but were soon to suffer the horrific slaughter at Chateau Thierry, St Mihiel, Pont A Mousson and so many other salient points in the Argonne.

Alice doubtlessly has played a very significant part in their long partnership and I am sure Parke does not need compliments or accolades from such as myself, but I would like to end this brief appraisal of Parke's memoirs with this reflection.

It has been my good fortune to have known many great men and women of our time and to have had entree to places and incidents that but for a lifetime of aviation, might not have been possible. In all that time, those I have admired the most have usually been quiet, modest individuals who seek neither fame nor fortune. They have their own code of conduct and behaviour. Parke, in my opinion, is a prime example and his reward has been the respect of his friends and the love, pride and admiration of his family.

Alex Henshaw MBE

Prologue

Something made me want to return; memories of the past, surely, but mostly curiosity about the present. Then, too, I had no one at home to talk to about the way it had been. They couldn't possibly understand how it felt to fly a Spitfire; to roll one over on its back and plummet thousands of feet in a matter of seconds, then swoop back up vertically, gracefully rolling along the way. I was asked, but I am sure I never satisfactorily explained the excitement, and the *esprit de corps*, or why I considered it a privilege to have risked my neck with such a courageous group of young men. Why go back? Nostalgia? Maybe. But whatever, I knew I must go.

It was 1954, eight years later, before it was possible. Alice and I took the train up from London and over to Chester, then a bus to the little hamlet of Hawarden that was a mile up the road above the airdrome. We had lunch in the old pub I used to frequent as a 'sprog' (new) Pilot Officer years before. It was much the same, although the old bartender was no longer with us.

Afterwards we strolled around town, admiring the narrow streets and the little stone houses until I realized I was subconsciously delaying the visit to No. 41 OTU. It was growing late when we began to descend the familiar hill that led past the old stone castle that had once been the WAAF officer's billets and on to the front gate.

The guard house was still there but no sentry to issue a challenge. All of the buildings, including the hangars as well as the roadways were still painted with the zigzagging dark green and brown wartime camouflage. The grass had been freshly mowed and there wasn't a scrap of paper or trash to be seen. The place was immaculate.

I peered through the window of my old hut and was astonished to see the bed was still made and the one chair, the table, the bureau, and the old stove with its three lumps of coal were still in their proper places. Standing there, I wondered how many men had lived in that same room and slept in that same bed, had survived.

The hangars were down the hill on the edge of the perimeter track. By the time we reached the first of those enormous buildings, the wind had picked up and it was getting cold. We still hadn't seen a living soul, and except for the wind, the only sound was the slamming of the unlocked entrance door. We stepped inside, not knowing what to expect. The interior was vacant, unbelievably clean, and except for the echo of the banging door, completely silent.

As we stood there shivering, I thought about the last time I had stood on this exact spot years before. The noise had been deafening. The hustle and bustle and chatter of the erks as they climbed over the aircraft, performing their jobs of refuelling, repair and maintenance, combined with the roar of the engines being tested, had looked and sounded like a well-orchestrated chaos. I just couldn't believe the silence. It was eerie.

We had turned to leave when I wondered if the control tower was open. Alice could get a spectacular view of the whole area. We tried the door and found it unlocked. We were halfway to the top of the stairs when I stopped. I thought I had heard the sound of voices. Deciding I must have imagined it, we continued our climb. I timidly opened a door marked 'Operations' and there sat two gentlemen, just as startled as we. They looked at us as though we were ghosts. Their first question was "Where the hell did you come from?"

My stammered explanation didn't impress them a bit. They didn't believe I had been stationed there until I described in detail the location of the flight sheds, the railroad tracks, the river to the north and other odds and ends about the station. Then they became quite friendly, offering us a cup of tea and giving Alice a tour of the tower and a view of the field itself. Their operation was being kept alive for research and development for the Bristol Aircraft Company, located across the field in the old Vickers Maintenance Unit hangars. The rest of the station was still the property of the RAF, which accounted for its excellent condition.

We thanked them for their kindness, told them good-bye, and caught the next bus back to Chester. All in all, the visit was interesting but depressing. I couldn't erase the memory of "the way it was."

The next day, we were sitting in Barlow's in Chester, one of England's oldest pubs and one of my favourite watering holes during the Hawarden days, when we decided to try to find the 'drome at Poulton. We drove out to where I knew it would be. I was sure, because there had been many nights when after the pubs had closed and the last bus had left, we would climb onto Ridgley's motorbike, as many as four of us, and weave our way back to the station in the pitch black night. With one on the rear fender, one on the handlebars, and two on the saddle seat, we must have looked like a circus act. Why we were not all killed remains a mystery. Ah well… at the time we were young and fearless and full of booze.

The old farmhouse was still there, but no sign of the airdrome. We asked several people, who admittedly, were quite young, but no one had ever heard of "Poulton Aerodrome". It had, no doubt, been turned back into what we were now seeing; a vast field of wheat, and long forgotten.

I wondered if we should continue our trek to the north, but after consultation with Alice, who had never before been to England or Scotland, we decided to press on, and took the overnight train to Inverness. We slept quite well and had a lovely breakfast next morning, a 'full English breakfast' of bacon, sausage, fried bread, fried egg, and potatoes, served at a table with a sparkling white tablecloth and, even though we were going at a pretty good clip, not a drop of tea was spilled as we raced around the curves. Those English trains were a wonder.

We hired a car and set off east for Peterhead. Our route took us near Banff and I had to stop to see if the old station for Beaufighters and Mosquitoes was still in existence. I never found it, but we did locate a small lane that led up to the edge of the cliffs that would have been nearby. We stopped and walked to the edge and looked out over that cold, gray, tumultuous sea. The view must have been the same the lads had seen when they took off and headed for the Norwegian and Danish coasts. I took a deep breath as I recalled the lucky escape Abbott and I had had when we finally found the lighted end of that fog-shrouded runway and again blessed those sodium lamps.

As we stood there I could almost hear the roar of those big Bristol engines on the Beaus and the high-pitched whine of the Merlins on the Mossies as they strained to take off, encumbered by their heavy loads of rockets and bombs. When mixed with the sound of the crashing waves below it must have been awesome.

The wind freshened and it started to rain; it was time to press on to Peterhead. We found what had been the entrance to the airdrome and followed the road to the narrow, dusty lane that formerly led to the mess. The little farm cottages, whose occupants used to hand us eggs in the morning darkness, still lined the road, some with their thatched roofs caved in, leaving nothing but a hollow shell. There was not a soul to be seen. The

Nissen hut that was once our billet was still there, looking rather forlorn with its windows dark and its door partly ajar, hanging loose on its hinges. I peeked in, then quickly withdrew. The entire hut was now used for the storage of cow manure!

We continued up the lane to what was previously a very proper, efficient station, one of the best, if not *the* best in Scotland. I was holding an old newspaper I had saved, the *Bon Accord* dated in 1945, and compared what I was looking at with photographs taken back then. They showed the two squadrons of Mustangs, their wings laden with extra fuel tanks, snaking along the perimeter track on their way to the active runway. In the background, one could see the well-arranged group of Quanset huts, hangars and administration buildings. The grass had been neatly trimmed and the control tower rose above it all.

But now it was a disaster! The administration building and the mess had collapsed, the tower had toppled and there was no sign that the hangars ever existed. The one remaining runway was reserved for drag racing and the rest of the area was now a rubbish dump for the city of Peterhead.

As we turned to go, I realized what the chap had meant when he said "One can never really go home again."

Parke F. Smith

Flight Lieutenant P.F. Smith RAFVR #134347

Preface

I was born in 1920. An early brush with disaster came when I was age five. My friends and I were playing "kick the can" late one afternoon. It was almost dark when I ran across the street chasing the can. First I heard it, then I looked up and saw it coming; a telephone repair truck. It could have snuffed out my lights permanently. I can still see clearly that black underbody with its muffler and exhaust pipe as the tire bumped over me. Some kind soul pulled my half-conscious body out of a sewer opening, placed me on the cool, leather back seat of an open-sided touring car and rushed me to the hospital.

I should have been scared, but all I could think of was how upset Mom and Dad were going to be with me for playing in the street at night. My brother James, two years older than I, had alerted everyone by running through the apartment screaming, "He's dead! He's dead!" They never told me whether his voice held a note of panic or joy. There were times when I suspected the latter. In any event he scared hell out of Mother and Father, but fortunately, I was found to have no damage other than an enormous lump on my head and a tire mark across my stomach.

A collision with a mail truck two years later almost did me in. It appeared out of a driveway concealed by a hedge, and I rammed it with my bicycle, flew over the hood and landed on my head and shoulder on a concrete sidewalk. I remained unconscious for hours. The bicycle was 'totalled' but once again I survived with no lasting damage.

As if this had not been enough, I managed to roll the family car over when I was thirteen but without major damage (other than to the car). I also managed to survive four and a half wartime years as a "friendly alien" in the Royal Air Force, where I was given the opportunity to, as RCAF Flight Lt John G. Magee Jr wrote – "dance the skies on laughter silvered wings."

But the most wonderful thing of all was meeting, falling in love with and marrying the most beautiful and wonderful girl in the world. Four lovely children and hordes of grandchildren have been the result. After fifty-three years, my heart still misses a beat when she walks into the room. How lucky can one be?

Parke F. Smith

Introduction

Dad had to quit school and go to work at age fourteen immediately after his father died in 1894. He worked his way up to be General Freight Agent of the Southern Railway before starting his own business, which was quite successful until the 1929 crash. His largest customer and several other companies failed, and their being unable to pay their bills left him in a desperate state. At the age of fifty, with a wife, three children and with heart trouble, he started all over again. Slowly but surely, he paid off each of his creditors and once again became financially secure. He taught me a lesson I never forgot: Never *ever* fail to pay your debts and continue to try, even when further effort seems hopeless.

The late twenties not only marked the beginning of a deep financial depression but also the beginning of the development of fixed-wing aircraft and I became fascinated by aviation. Aerial demonstrations and pulp magazines were responsible for keeping my interest at fever pitch. *War Birds, Aces of the Air,* etc, as well as the comic strip *Tailspin Tommy* and others – all dealing with exploits in World War I – were required reading at my age, much of it under the bed covers at night with the aid of a flashlight. Spads, Sopwith Camels, Se5s, Jenneys, Fokker D7s and D8s, and Gotha Bombers were the usual subjects. The writers' descriptions of how the pilots manipulated the throttle, the rudder bars and control column were in such detail that, by the age of ten, I was quite sure that I could fly and easily perform loops, chandelles, Immelmanns and flare-out for landing with the best of them.

Every day there was something new. The huge German flying boat, the DO-X landed in Baltimore Harbour one summer day in 1926. Dad and I watched as the behemoth, almost hidden by spray, taxied up to the dock where we stood. The noise of those twelve engines was something a young lad could never forget!

The following year Charles Lindbergh made his historic flight over the Atlantic to Paris and was given a hero's welcome upon his return. I watched as he was driven down one of the main streets of Baltimore, grinning and waving as he sat up on the back of a long black touring car.

A few months after his record achievement, the world's largest rigid airship, the Graf Zeppelin, flew overhead as I was walking to school early one morning – an enormous cigar-shape floating soundlessly in the still air, low enough that I could see almost every detail – the ridges in the envelope, the passenger cabin and the long, trailing ropes used to guide and secure the monster to its mooring mast.

One Sunday, in order to preserve Mother's sanity, Father had the duty to entertain his young son somewhere other than in the house. He drove me in our brand new Rio Flying Cloud roadster (with a "rumble seat" in back) out into the country to what was billed as a "County Air Fair." The details of that exposition are rather hazy, but I do recall that the grand finale featured a fellow hanging by his knees from a trapeze suspended below a hot air balloon. There was a gasp from the crowd as he let go and fell for several hundred feet before deploying a parachute.

Later that same summer, I was sent off to Camp Gunston in the hills of Pennsylvania on the edge of a beautiful, blue-water lake. Canoeing, archery, shooting, horseback riding, etc, were all mandatory. I can't say it was fun – I was homesick a good part of the time – but it certainly was an experience.

My first encounter with horses left something to be desired. I was told to mount up on a pony named 'Maryland'. As I was climbing into the saddle, he turned his head and gave me about as nasty a look as I had ever seen. I should have paid more attention to what he was trying to tell me... We were led out of the paddock by a groom, who handed me the reins as he stepped back. As soon as the beast realized he was free and had a neophyte clinging to his miserable withers, he took off for the apple orchard at full gallop with his 'driver' screaming "Whoa!" at the top of his lungs. Precious little good it did. The beggar shot under a low-hanging branch – I just *knew* he had done this before! It whacked me on the side of the head and I was unhorsed, out like a light, on what was my first, and last, attempt.

That afternoon at dusk I headed for the paddock in search of an older friend, one of the grooms, who was usually mucking out the stables at the end of the day. Picking my way through mud and piles of manure I suddenly heard the crashing and splashing of hoofs. I looked up just as an enormous beast charged over me, flattening me into the mire and manure before disappearing over the fence. Having heard the commotion, my friend appeared, dragged me to my feet and proceeded to berate me for being so stupid. But how was I to know that one should never walk in front of a horse at night? I didn't even know the darned thing was there! Why anyone would want to fool around with these critters was beyond me. That was more than seventy years ago but I still remember the horse's name – who could ever forget 'Scoofer'!

Two days later it was discovered that my roommate had contracted polio. It was announced that the camp was to be burned to the ground and our parents were to pick us up in the morning. Dad arrived and we were about to leave when a large twin-engine amphibian landed on the lake to pick up Admiral Moffet's son, a fellow-camper. As it took off in a sheet of spray and disappeared over the trees, I thought:

"Now that's the way to go!"

1. A Construction Effort

One of the older lads in the neighbourhood (no more than fourteen) started to build a three-quarter-scale British Se5 World War I biplane in his father's garage. With the understanding that I would be allowed to taxi it at least once, I was enlisted as chief scrounger for the necessary wood strips from a lumber yard about a half mile away. The sight of a small boy making frequent trips to and from the lumber yard, dragging strips of 2 x 2 x 12 white pine along a busy thoroughfare, across streetcar tracks and into a rather exclusive neighbourhood, for some reason didn't seem to attract the attention of the foot patrolman walking our beat. I wondered how long it would be before the lumber yard began to question what was happening to their stock. Subsequently, I learned that the manager had followed me almost to the job-site, and was well aware of the project. This explained the sudden appearance of a pile of two-by-twos next to the entrance of the yard and some very nominal bills my father received, but never mentioned until years later.

Construction continued in the afternoons after school and on weekends for at least six months before it began to resemble an airplane. The young builder's father was a real help, securing pipe for the landing gear, wheels from a retired motorbike, an old wooden propeller, and best of all, an engine from a junked Model T Ford. His mother did the cutting and sewing of the old linen bed sheets that were later sewn to the wing ribs and "doped" with banana oil.

I remember seeing this creation, engine, prop and undercart installed, no wings, no covering on the fuselage, headed down the street with its throttle wide open, the unmuffled engine roaring, the prop barely turning, and the designer-engineer and project manager seated proudly on a board seat. Unfortunately, our neighbors didn't share our enthusiasm for aeronautics and raised such a "stink" the project had to be abandoned. The "chief pilot" headed off to boarding school. I was crushed. My only hope of taxiing a real airplane had vanished.

I remained in a funk until a short time later when the father of a friend invited my brother and me to Logan Field, in Baltimore, where he had arranged as a birthday gift for his son, flights for us all in a new Curtis Robin. That did it.

That fifteen minute aerial tour of the city sealed my fate. I *had* to fly!

The Author, on the way to the lumber yard.

2. Taking Wing

I was not much of a student, but I did manage to stagger through public high school and a year of private school before heading for college. One of my classmates was my good friend David Satterfield, III, whose father, US Congressman David Satterfield Jr, would three years later provide me with the confidential information that would put me in touch with the Royal Air Force (RAF).

It was now 1939 and I had just read about a young British aviator, Alex Henshaw, who had flown in a small, single-engined racing plane, alone, from Gravesend, just outside London, to Cape Town South Africa and returned in 76 hours 48 minutes. This was over desert, sea and jungle with no radio aids; only a compass and a self-made strip-map. A fete of courage and navigational skill that set a record that stands unbroken today, more than 60 years later. What an inspiration for us young fledglings! He later became Chief Test Pilot for Supermarine Aircraft Co., and during the war, tested most of the Spitfires, and many other types of aircraft. He is alive and well today, and a very dear friend.

At the University of Virginia, I was barely able to keep up during the first year, and the second year became a disaster. My scholastic troubles increased tenfold when the University started flight training under the Civil Pilot Training Program. It consisted of a complete ground school course and thirty hours of flying, enough for me to qualify for a private pilot's license. The total cost was $150. This was a princely sum in those days, but

Father managed it, even though he suspected it would be the death knell for my studies. As usual, he was right. However, in later years he confessed it was one of the best financial investments he had ever made. I was forced to agree!

Ground school was at the University. There were three two-hour sessions every week, and if one failed, he didn't get a second chance, he was immediately dropped from the program. That was incentive enough. I passed with flying colours!

The flying field was ten miles east of Charlottesville, and as there was no public transportation, we had to rely on one of our "happy band" who was far richer than we, and the owner of a new Packard Phaeton. It would cruise at ninety, as he was always eager to demonstrate, scaring the hell out of the rest of us. (Four years later in North Africa, I picked up an old issue of the international *Time* magazine and noticed an article describing an accident at a railway crossing. The car was going at such a high rate of speed that it derailed the locomotive. I was not surprised to learn that it was the same lad.)

Piper Cubs were used for flight training. They were fabric-covered, steel-framed, high-wing monoplanes. Painted in their trademark yellow, they looked like toys. The propeller was wooden and the engine was a Franklin four-cylinder, sixty-horsepower piece of efficiency rarely known to fail. The fuel gauge, located just forward of the windscreen, was a foot-long length of wire stuck in a cork float in the tank. The wire protruded through a hole in the fuel cap, and the height of the wire indicated the amount of fuel on board. How simple can a design be? Entrance to the cockpit was through two horizontal doors, the upper one hinged along the top and the lower hinged along the bottom. This allowed them to be opened in flight, which was mighty nice on a hot summer day.

Jim Beverage, my instructor, was a nice, quiet, well-mannered and handsome young fellow. With his light hair, sunburned and weathered face, he was the very image of a pilot without trying to be. He was also an excellent teacher; without yelling or screaming he managed to lead me through all the do's and don'ts of the basics so efficiently that I was allowed to go solo after only seven hours.

The elation of that first solo flight is hard to describe. How awe-inspiring it was to look down from eight hundred or a thousand feet with the realization that I, and I alone, was responsible for getting the thing *and myself* back on the ground in one piece. This was accomplished to the applause of Mr Beverage and the few of my fellow-students who still remained in the course. (Several had dropped out due to ground school troubles, lack of interest, or personal reasons.) This solo flight was the beginning of a love affair that was to last for fifty years.

Ground school and the required thirty flying hours completed, I was awarded my private pilot's license in May 1940.

3. Marking Time

Retired from the University that summer, I flew passengers on a "Ten Dollar ~ Ten Minute" ride at the local Crestview Airport on weekends, accepting the flying time as payment. It was a wonderful way to build up time for free.

Brother James had graduated from Virginia Military Institute (VMI), joined the Navy, and at the time was instructing at Pensacola Naval Air Station in Florida. Home on leave, he *had* to try the Piper Cub. It had the characteristic of "floating" forever if a landing was attempted at anything even slightly faster than its thirty mile per hour stalling speed. After three attempts he gave up, and turned it over to his little brother. He took it all in good grace, but I am forced to confess, I was more than a little proud.

I worked for Father that fall. My job was to call on various building contractors and superintendents and try to persuade them to do business with us. There was a rather large federal housing project underway nearby and I had called on the superintendent numerous times without success. I was sure he "had his hand out," but Father had impressed upon me that we were not to offer anything other than entertainment when in pursuit of a job.

One morning this prospective customer happened to mention that he enjoyed deep sea fishing off the Outer Banks of North Carolina, but there wasn't enough time to drive all that way on a weekend and get back to work by Monday morning. I offered to fly him down and back if he would pay half the rental and fuel for the aircraft. He jumped at it. I chartered a little two-seated

Taylorcraft, and we left for Cape Hatteras the next Saturday morning.

My aerial chart didn't indicate an airfield on the Cape, but he told me he had seen airplanes land in the sand in front of the hotel numerous times, and, naively, I thought he knew what he was talking about. We arrived, landed in the sand in front of a dilapidated and deserted hotel, and went fishing on a boat that he had chartered and paid for.

When the time came to leave at three o'clock on Sunday afternoon, to my dismay, the little Taylorcraft wouldn't budge in the soft sand. My passenger jumped out and returned a few minutes later dragging a couple of ten-foot boards, which he stuck under the wheels. After letting a little air out of the tires and bouncing over the sand for what seemed like hours, we became unstuck and were airborne.

Low on fuel now, and unable to do anything about it, I said nothing, and with grave misgivings, set course across Albermarle Sound, hoping to make it to the opposite shore. I felt we had enough to reach Elizabeth City but had no idea where we would land unless we illegally used the Naval Air Station nearby on the Pasquotank River.

The shoreline came in sight, but an adverse wind had picked up and things became rather "hairy" as the wire on the fuel gauge cap reached its limit, indicating "Empty." I decided to put it down on the Naval base before the engine quit, and was turning downwind when my passenger pointed to a grass field just below that had aircraft parked in front of some buildings. Throttled back, with the prop barely ticking over, we glided onto the runway.

As I opened the throttle to taxi back, the engine gave its last gasp. We were out of fuel.

We climbed out and were immediately surrounded by a group of people, who insisted on pinning little American flags on our sweaters. This was the opening day of the new Elizabeth City Airport, and they thought a "deadstick" landing was part of the entertainment!

We spent the night in a nearby motel, arose early Monday morning, and made it back to Richmond in time for work. Father called me from the office a few hours later to say we had just received the order for the project – our largest ever up to that time. I was amused by the thought that my customer had paid for half the aircraft rental, half the fuel, all of the boat, motel and breakfast charges, and neither of us had caught a single fish. Yet he said he had a really great time! (Ignorance is bliss!)

4. Aerobatics

By winter I had earned enough to enrol in the Civil Aeronautics Authority's (CAA) advanced flying course at Richmond's Byrd Field, under Chief Instructor Vernon "Squeak" Burnett, one of the finest aerobatic pilots in the country. The course consisted of twenty-five hours of aerobatic instruction in an old Waco RNF biplane, and a beautiful aluminium low-wing monoplane, the Ryan STA. The Waco had a radial Warner engine and the Ryan, an inline, inverted Monasco.

It was the dead of winter, cold as all get out, and, as both planes had open cockpits, at times we were so miserable we almost gave up. My good friend, John Fleming, myself, and three others persevered and completed the course, but not without considerable hollering and screaming from Squeak.

An intercom called a "Gosport", was the only means of communication between the front and rear cockpits. This consisted of two small hose-pipes with a funnel attached on one end, and earphones on the other, the earphones being connected to one's helmet. There were times when it sounded as though Squeak was crawling right through the darned thing to join me in the rear. My main instructor was, thankfully, Gwenn "Wen" Colby, a tall, calm, quiet fellow, but Squeak was chief, and he was "antsy" and tough as nails. All of five foot four, he would at times become so enraged that he would appear to swell up to at least six foot six.

One icy morning at three thousand feet he shouted, "Is your seat belt tight?" Having no idea what he was up to, and being rather casual about flying with my seat belt only comfortably snug, I slipped my hand under the belt to be sure it was fastened and replied in the affirmative. With that, the little beggar flipped the Waco on its back. I shot out of the cockpit and dangled there by the belt, in a "U" shape, up to my waist in the slipstream. The fuel tank was located in the upper wing and fuel was pouring out of the air vent. He held this position for at least thirty seconds, until I was thoroughly soaked, then rolled it upright, and then, very sweetly, asked if my belt was still tight!

That winter was an especially cold one, with snow on the ground most of the time. As we started at six a.m., long before sunup, there were times we hated to leave the warmth of the hangar and climb into an open cockpit. But it was the only way to escape Squeak's verbal abuse.

Spring finally came and the rest of the course was a sheer delight. One can never forget those soft, warm, misty April mornings at dawn. The air was very still at times and, since there was no control tower, we could take off in either direction. The only hazard was the early morning arrival of the Eastern Airlines flight from Washington DC; its wheels would still be down because it took too long to hand crank them up for such a short flight. It would appear in the mist just over the treetops, headed for a landing to the south, while we were taking off to the north on the same runway. No one panicked; each simply moved to the right and waved a greeting as we passed. Try to imagine *that* taking place today without the hue and cry of a dozen federal agencies! This aerobatic training proved to be invaluable later. Not only did it improve my ability to recover from unusual attitudes, it opened the door to learning many manoeuvres used in combat that were to save my life on more than one occasion.

With the required number of hours of the course completed, I decided to try my luck with the Naval Air Corps, and an appointment was made through a local recruiter for a medical exam at Anacostia Naval Air Station near Washington, D.C.

5. Rejected

I arrived in Washington at 6:00 am as scheduled, after a three-hour drive from Richmond. I joined a queue of a hundred or more bare-chested young applicants, and as the line snaked back and forth, I came face to face with my old St. Christopher's chum, Dave Satterfield. He was headed in the opposite direction, and we barely had time to speak. I wasn't to see him again until many years after the war when, following in his father's footsteps, he was elected to the U.S. House of Representatives. (Dave had a remarkable experience which was written up as the lead story in the national magazine, *The Saturday Evening Post*. He crash-landed on the flight deck of his carrier despite being badly wounded and with his Hellcat almost unflyable.)

The first Medical Officer (MO) took my blood pressure, and passed me along for a multitude of other tests that took until 3:00 pm, when I was told to "pack it up." I had failed, due to a physical deformity and high blood pressure. These were the results from the *first two* tests I had taken at 6:00 in the morning! I was told to have the deformity repaired and return to try again.

Dr. Carrington Williams, a surgeon and good friend, who was at that time head of the Army's 45th General Hospital, performed the rather painful operation. I returned for re-examination, only to be told by a very young Navy doctor that he didn't consider the operation a success and added I would probably be classified "4F", i.e. unfit for military service. I had the good sense to ask him to put it in writing. He did so, reluctantly, and I headed to the nearest public telephone.

I called Dave's father, told him the story, and asked him to tell me all he knew about the British RAF recruiting scheme. He gave me the name of the Canadian Aviation Board, located in New York City at the Waldorf Astoria Hotel, with the request that I keep the source of the information confidential. With the Navy doctor's letter of rejection, my pilot's log book, and the $50 I had left after paying for my train ticket, I headed for New York. I arrived about 9:00 pm.

Next day, at the Waldorf, I found that this clandestine recruiting operation was run by a very pleasant British gentleman, Mr Fairfax H. Gouverneur. He was unable to see me until late that afternoon. After a few minutes of conversation, he said there was little hope as the last class for flight instruction had been formed and was on its way to California. My disappointment was apparent. However, when I mentioned something about my pilot's license going to waste, he showed immediate interest. As long as I wouldn't require initial flight training, he would try to have me enrolled in the last "refresher class", provided I passed a flight test and a medical examination.

By now it was 4:00 pm, but he put in a call to a "Doctor Ray" with the request that he see me immediately. The doctor's office was on the tenth floor of an apartment building on Park Avenue. A ten-minute cab ride left me standing on the curb in front of his address with no idea what I was getting into. He would have to be a wizard to complete a medical exam by 5:00 pm, even if he only performed half the number of tests the Navy had.

The building was typical of Park Avenue apartments; built around a hollow centre that served as an air shaft, and provided light to the inside rooms. Dr Ray's office was about twenty feet square. It had a chair and one window directly behind his desk. A small alcove held a black box containing two little sticks. One was supposed to line these up to check depth perception. A washstand and numerous photographs on the walls completed the room's contents.

I introduced myself, and he told me he had been waiting for me, and said, "Let's get down to business." He checked my eyesight by asking me to read an eye chart from about ten feet away. He didn't comment when I complied with both eyes open.

He listened to my chest with his naked ear, made me line up the two little sticks, and then asked me to lean over with trousers at half mast. Grunting approval, he handed me a small glass, indicated the sink, and requested a urine sample. He was seated at his desk when I handed him the results of my efforts. Accepting the nearly full glass, he turned in his chair, held it up to the light, stared at it for a brief moment and said "Looks all right to me," and with that, poured it out the open window down the air shaft! Then he scribbled a few notes, and called Mr Gouverneur to say that I had passed!

I looked at my watch and saw that the entire examination had taken exactly forty minutes. Comparing this with the Navy's exam, I decided he either had a "hot date" or didn't want to miss "happy hour."

As I was leaving, I again noticed the photographs. They were all autographed with such inscriptions as: "To Dr. Ray, Admiral Richard E. Byrd"; "All the best, James Doolittle"; "To my good friend, Dr. Ray, Roscoe Turner"; and so on. I learned that he was the only CAA licensed medical examiner in New York City, and any pilot in the area whose medical required renewal, had to use his services.

I telephoned Gouverneur and caught him just as he was leaving his office. He congratulated me and told me a flight test had been arranged for 6:00 am the next morning. I was to report to Speed Hanson's Flying Service at Flushing Meadows Airport. This was out in the marshes, just off what is now the main east-west runway of LaGuardia Airport. I believe it is still in operation today.

A room at the McAlpin Hotel was $15 in those days and the taxi fare to and from the airfield was $3. My $50 was going fast, but I was so elated at the prospect of maybe, *just maybe,* being accepted by the RAF that I really didn't care, and I had a big steak for dinner.

I called Dad that night, collect. He was more than a little surprised to learn I was in New York instead of Washington, and headed for the RAF, not the Navy. We decided to withhold that news from Mother until my return when things would be more definite.

I arrived at Speed Hanson's Flying Service early the next morning, in time to watch the sun rising over a deserted airfield, a rather ramshackle hangar, and a well-worn grass airstrip. "Speed" drove up a few moments later, introduced himself and congratulated me for being prompt. We strolled over to the hangar and struggled to get the sagging door open. When I saw what was inside, I almost wished the door had stuck shut. It was the biggest biplane I had ever seen; a giant Eagle Rock with a huge in-line OX5 water-cooled engine, complete with radiator cap! The propeller was at least ten feet in diameter, and while I don't recall the RPM, in flight it was so slow one could almost count each turn. The two of us, unaided, pushed it out to the flight line.

Speed was nice enough, but offered little in the way of instruction or encouragement. The cockpit was so big I actually had to lean way forward just to reach the control column, and stretch my legs as far as possible to even touch the rudder-bar. The designer must have been a very large man.

The throttle and mixture controls were in the right place, but again, at arm's length. He showed me the magneto switches, then jumped down off the wing, went around and called "Contact," then swung the prop by hand. The engine caught with a belch of black smoke. He climbed in and said, "It's all yours, let's go." Big help! Well, it was his airplane and if he didn't mind, I surely didn't.

The wide, soft undercarriage made taxiing fairly simple. I lined up into the little bit of wind there was, took a good look around to see how high we sat when on the ground, and as I eased open the throttle, we began to move slowly across the grass. Not daring to take my eyes off the horizon to check the airspeed indicator, I could only wait for the tail to lift and the controls to become lighter in order to feel when it was ready to fly. It came unstuck at no more than fifty miles an hour, and we gradually climbed to 1,000 feet, turning slightly from side to side to make certain there was nothing ahead. We had made one wide circle over one of the bridges in the East River when Speed signalled for me to land. The moment of truth had arrived.

I could see the airfield some distance ahead and slowly began a descent. Once over the hedgerows, we levelled off to what I thought was the proper height, and I waited for what seemed an eternity. I was thinking that I must have miscalculated, and really blown it, when I suddenly realized that we were no longer descending but slowing down as the tail was beginning to drag. The undercarriage was so soft and the wheels so large it was almost impossible to feel the touchdown. What a relief! I knew he would want to do it again and was holding my breath, but he indicated we were to return to the hangar.

He shut down the engine and I remained seated, praying he would say the right thing, but as he climbed out he asked where I was from. I told him and he laughed and said, "Nice landing. It's a good thing you are from the South. When I felt the controls shaking, I thought you were very anxious or scared and that wouldn't do. I recognized your accent and decided you were cold. I'll call Gouverneur and tell him you are acceptable." I never corrected him, and was relieved that he took no notice of my perspiration.

I "floated" back to the hotel and found a note from Gouverneur telling me I would be the last to join the final class of trainees, and that I should wait at home for airline tickets to Los Angeles, which would be telegraphed in a few days. The "refresher course" was to be held at a private flight training school for the RAF's War Eagle Field at Lancaster, California.

I was a nervous wreck for a long ten days, but the ticket finally arrived along with a check for travel expenses. These people were trusting souls! I had signed nothing, was still a civilian, and would remain so until I arrived in London six months later to take an oath of loyalty to the King.

In those days a government priority was required for travel and it wasn't unusual for some people to wait for days or even weeks before getting a seat on an airplane. All I had was the telegram instructing me to report a.s.a.p. to Lancaster. I managed a flight from Richmond to Washington, but there I was stuck. After many futile pleas to the airline agent, I was about to give up. A chap in shirtsleeves who had been walking back and forth behind the counter stopped, and said he had overheard the conversation and asked if he could help. He looked at my telegram and then disappeared into a nearby office, only to reappear a few minutes later with a handful of boarding passes and his calling card. On it was a note to the manager of Midway Airport. He had gotten me a seat to Chicago and told me to show the card to Midway's manager upon arrival.

I boarded the next flight about 6:00 pm. It was one of the early model DC3's and when it started to rain and hail over West Virginia, the noise in that lightly insulated metal cabin was incredible. By the time we reached Chicago it was dark, and the poor visibility had forced us so low that, in fact, we were flying just slightly above the street lights that reflected in the rain-slicked streets. It was a real thrill to see the top of a gas storage tank whiz by at eye level!

We landed at about midnight, and I headed straight for the manager's office and showed him the card. He seemed impressed, and after very little conversation, I had clearance all the way to Los Angeles, via Tennessee, back up to Indiana, down to Arizona and over to California. I can't recall the number of stops or plane changes, but it took twenty-one hours to get there.

I wrote my benefactor a thank-you note and several years after the war I learned that he had been promoted to head one of our largest airlines.

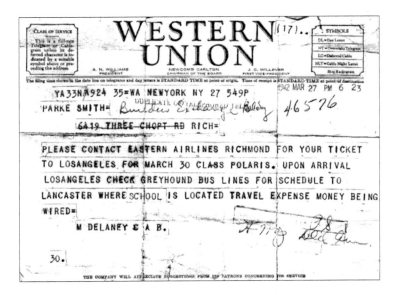

6. A Refresher Course

I had heard about California but had never been there, and was duly impressed by the palm trees, lack of crowds, warm sunny climate, pretty girls (not an ugly one in sight), and the orange juice stands on practically every corner. One could buy a big glass of juice for five cents.

Having grown up in Virginia, I had lived among and associated with black people all my life. I was puzzled when I stepped off the train to see a crowd gathered around an American soldier. Curious, I asked one of the bystanders the reason for the commotion. "Look. He's a black man!" was the reply. When visiting Los Angeles today it is hard to believe that most of the people in California in 1942 had never before seen a Negro.

A Greyhound bus took me the last sixty miles to Lancaster. A very small town, it contained a bar, a drugstore, a small general store and a railroad station. The evening amusement for the locals was to stand as close to the track as possible, and revel in the blast of cooling air as the Santa Fe Super Chief rushed through at eighty miles an hour.

Polaris (War Eagle Field) was about five miles to the east, on the edge of the Mojave Desert. The trip, on a rickety local bus, offered my first glimpse of sagebrush, tumble weeds and the endless expanse of sand and dust that was the desert. Air conditioning was far in the future and the bus, under the noonday sun, became unbearably hot. The few other passengers and I hung out of the windows as we bumped and ground along the narrow, dusty, unpaved lane imprisoned by cattle fences on both sides.

I had often heard of the bird called a "road runner" but had never seen one. We were travelling at twenty miles an hour at least, and this funny little creature, looking just like a skinny rooster, red cockscomb and all, was keeping up right alongside, legs a blur, going like pistons. It kept pace for almost a quarter of a mile before it suddenly had to make a lifesaving swerve to avoid the gate post at the base. It shot through an opening in the fence and was soon lost in the distance, legs still a-going.

I was met by a blast of even hotter air as I stepped off the bus, and dragged my bags over to what looked like a guard house. A watchman on duty was kind enough to lead me over to one of several very clean, white, one-story bungalows surrounded by lush green grass. The Sierra Nevada Mountains to the west made a beautiful backdrop.

Inside, the "hut" was made up of four two-bed rooms and one bath and it was stifling hot. He turned on one of the most efficient air conditioners I had ever seen. It was a box, mounted on the wall up next to the ceiling. It was exposed to the outdoors and filled with excelsior moistened by a spray of water. When an enclosed fan was turned on, blowing hot, dry, outside air over the contents, the high rate of evaporation had the room chilled in a very few minutes.

There were ten or twelve of these huts and a long, low building containing the mess hall and the administration offices. In addition, there were three huge hangars next to a control tower, with aircraft parked in front. My roommate-to-be, Fred Hill, arrived along with several others, who were billeted in the other three rooms. Everyone was dressed in the blue coveralls that were to become our uniform for the next six weeks

Twelve of us were in the class, and a "motley crew" we were. Only two of us, Bill Braun and I, were not ex-Army or Navy. The others had been dismissed from the armed services for one reason or another, mostly for rule infractions or disciplinary reasons. However, they had to have passed a flight test or they wouldn't have been there. Apart from a class of twenty RAF cadets, we were all civilians as were the flight instructors.

We didn't have to endure military training, only flight testing and ground school. Ground school was fun. We were taught how the British were doing things. Their terminology was strange at first, but after putting it to use we found that it made sense, and was very practical. Radio procedures, navigation, mechanics, theory of flight, and meteorology all took the better part of the first week, and then the flying began.

Flight training consisted of ten hours in the Stearman, two at night; fifteen hours in the BT13, four at night; and twenty hours in the AT 6, four at night. As one advanced, the type of aircraft used was a little more sophisticated than its predecessor, but the transition was not very difficult. The AT 6 was the only one with a retractable undercarriage, and that kept us on our toes, but it was a delight to fly aerobatically.

Aerobatic manoeuvres were performed over the 5000 ft. high mountains. As we were not allowed to go below five thousand feet above ground level, we had to start at thirteen to fifteen thousand feet above sea level. We did this routinely with no oxygen. I never heard anyone complain, but I doubt if that would be allowed today.

Night flying was most enjoyable. We would begin about 10 pm, and fly until first light. Only two aircraft would be in the circuit at one time. We were brought sandwiches and coffee at midnight. Lying in the grass on a cool desert night watching the wing-tip lights up against the stars, listening to the squeal of tires on the runway, and commenting on the quality of each landing, was magical and well worth a night of lost sleep.

Huge tumble weeds were a problem. They would break loose in the slightest breeze, and come rolling down the runway two or more at a time. These menaces were as much as eight to ten feet in diameter, and a real hazard night and day.

We were paid $30 a week with $10 deducted for laundry. It cost at least $40 to spend a night in Hollywood on a weekend off. Some didn't save up, and those in the most desperate need, would retire to the nearest hut after pay parade, spread a blanket on one of the beds, stretch it tight as a drum, and start the fastest crap game known to man. No time was wasted. One's $20 hit the bed and was rolled for. The winner retired with his $40 and thoughts of forty-eight hours of debauchery in "Tinsel Town." The loser faced a dreary weekend on the base.

Doug Munson, a friend from the class ahead, took me to town to show me the "ropes," and I must say, Hollywood was as described. As mentioned before, not a plain or unattractive girl in sight. They were all perfectly beautiful, each hoping to be discovered by some talent scout for the films. Munson was a handsome fellow, a dead ringer for Douglas Fairbanks, Jr. We walked into a bar dressed in "civvies" (but wearing our flying jackets) and were immediately surrounded by a bevy of beauties. Doug let it be known that he worked for MGM studios and they *just knew* he was a talent scout and I, his assistant; an assumption neither of us made any attempt to refute.

The little gathering soon became a party of sailors, marines, army airmen, etc., with not a male civilian in sight other than Doug and me. They kept telling the ladies how terribly difficult military life was, and how fortunate we were to be civilians. Of course, we sympathized deeply, and announced that we were to be drafted almost any day now, and in the meantime, were attending flight school on our own. This brought forth round after round of fresh drinks paid for by our new-found friends.

At about four-thirty in the morning the barkeeper announced the bar would close at five o'clock for cleaning, and would re-open at six. At this announcement, everyone got a fresh drink, and moved outside. I'll never forget the spectacle of forty or fifty people in uniforms and cocktail dresses (Doug and I in flying jackets), drinks in hand, sitting on the curb in front of a bar at the entrance to one of Hollywood's finest hotels at the now famous intersection of Hollywood and Vine. At six on the dot, we all stood up and marched back inside to continue the party. Apparently, this was a daily routine!

Smith and Hill – War Eagle Field 1940.

By nine o'clock that morning, we were in pretty bad shape, so after telling everyone good-bye and promising the ladies we would be in touch, we headed for the nearest White Tower restaurant. I remember sitting at the counter trying my best to face up to a cup of coffee, when a fellow seated beside me ordered two fried eggs and a piece of strawberry shortcake with lots of whipped cream; when the order arrived, darned if he didn't put the two fried eggs on top of the whipped-cream-covered berries and pour catsup over the lot. He then proceeded to devour the mess. When he cut into the eggs, things got a little hazy and I "lost it." Doug would never say exactly what had happened next, other than that we had been forcibly ejected by a waiter and several bystanders.

Polaris Academy at War Eagle Field. The author (3rd from left) was the only one to make it into the RAF.

7. Flight Training

We began working our way through the three stages; primary, basic and advanced. There were only three accidents I can recall that were serious. The first was when a lad was low-flying along the floor of one of the canyons in Nevada, and came to a turn, and a dead end. Not having enough room to turn or enough speed to climb out, he went headlong into the canyon wall. There was much discussion as to the best way out of such a situation, and it was decided that, with enough speed and aerobatic ability, one could do half of a Cuban eight to reverse one's course a hundred and eighty degrees. (The Cuban eight is three quarters of a loop with a half roll on the down side.) However, even if this lad had the speed, he lacked the aerobatic training.

The second was when one of the chaps was trying to land a Stearman. He applied too much brake after touchdown, and nosed over on his back. He hung there uninjured, but wanting to make an exit as quickly as possible, he released his seat belt, fell three feet onto his head, and broke his neck, yet he survived.

The third was an even greater tragedy. One of the British cadets was walking in front of a row of parked aircraft, head down, reading a letter from home. There was so much noise from the engines and turning propellers, and his concentration on the letter was so intense, he walked unseeingly into one of the propellers.

Our instructors were a mixed bag; some ex-army, a few ex-crop dusters and/or bush pilots, and one elderly gentleman, Mr. Hutton, a fifty-five year old who had seen one of his pupils shot down when caught flying a Piper Cub during a Japanese raid. At the time, he was chief instructor at a small field near Hickam Field in Honolulu. All of these instructors, with one exception, were now civilians and wore Army coveralls with their rank insignias painted black. The exception was RAF Wing Commander Greeves, in his RAF uniform. He was the final check pilot, and judged whether you passed or failed the course.

My favorites were Mr. Hutton, an excellent instructor, and Mr Grimsley. Grimsley, a tall, slightly built ex-bush pilot with a dry sense of humour, was a real master of the Stearman. He was determined to make sure everyone was well drilled in aerobatics, and my previous training with Squeak Burnett and Wen Colby went a long way toward cementing our friendship. His written assessment of my flying ability, not usually revealed to a student, was secretly shown to me by our Adjutant. These reports were long, detailed summaries of a student's abilities or lack thereof. On mine he had written laconically, "This student can simulate any manoeuvre shown." A real compliment!

When we had only a few hours of training remaining to complete the course, it was decided to move us to the newly constructed "Avenger Field" in Sweetwater, Texas. We were now the last class in this British scheme. Munson's class, the one ahead of us, had graduated just before we left Lancaster, and we were going to be the only group stationed at this huge complex.

The afternoon before we were going to leave, I was in town at the drug store riffling through magazines while waiting for my roommate, Fred, when I noticed the cover of the national magazine, *Redbook*. It was adorned with the photo of a very handsome, eager-looking aviation cadet in full flying garb, including helmet and goggles, standing at attention and saluting, against the background of the American flag. It was my old friend and ex-roommate at the University of Virginia, T. Todd Dabney. Apparently he had been chosen by his commanding officer at Mitchell Field, where he was stationed, to represent all the flying-cadets – quite an honour.

Fred and I and several others flew the AT 6's to Sweetwater via El Paso, Texas, where we were to refuel. One of the aircraft became unserviceable and it was decided to spend the night in El Paso's Hotel del Norte. The weather was steaming and we were hot, sweaty, and badly in need of a bath.

As we registered, I heard my named called, and to my astonishment, a beautiful, fresh as a daisy young lady ran across the lobby and gave me a big hug. An old friend who had been at nearby Sweetbriar when I was at the University of Virginia, she had just arrived from Virginia and was waiting to be met by her sister. She was a very shapely, pretty girl, and the looks on the faces of my companions watching the action, was something to behold. Unfortunately, her sister arrived while I was up in the room trying to clean up, and she was whisked off, never to be seen again. I understand that today she is happily married and lives in North Carolina.

We reached Avenger Field the next day and were told our quarters were not quite ready. We were released for a week with instructions to be back on time, or else... I had saved enough for a round-trip ticket from nearby Abeline and caught the next flight out to Richmond.

It was good to see the family again, but when it came time to return, just two days before my sister's wedding, I had a hard time explaining why I couldn't stay when, as they put it, I wasn't in the "real" armed forces, and could leave whenever I so desired. But I wasn't about to endanger the opportunity I had worked so hard for, and, secretly, I missed the flying. It took years for them to forgive me.

Sweetwater, Texas was a sleepy little desert town with no more than two or three thousand people, one of whom was the brother of General Claire Chaunault of the famous Flying Tigers Squadron. I met him when I was trying to send a telegram. He was the telegrapher for Western Union.

Training proceeded at a faster pace than at Lancaster, and we were told it was because of a very special course that was to begin as soon as we graduated. There was a shortage of instructors. Many of those who had taught at Lancaster, being civilians, had chosen to go elsewhere, and I was happy to accept their offer to be an aerobatic assistant, and help those who were lagging behind. I could always use that extra flying time.

Early one morning, I was in the back seat of an AT 6 with one of my fellow-students in front, preparing to take off to practice Cuban eights. These require some inverted or "negative G" positions. He had been doing these solo and having problems. We took off and after reaching altitude, cleared the area. As we started up a half loop, I glanced down under the instrument panel into the forward cockpit. His unfastened seatbelts were dangling loose. We were able to stop the manoeuvre in time, but had he been alone, and inverted the aircraft, he would more than likely have fallen into the canopy with disastrous results.

We finished our training, successfully completed a flight check with Wing Commander Greeves, and were graduated with very little fanfare. A photograph was taken of the class and we each received a copy as well as a ticket to Ottawa, Ontario, Canada, and $50 for expenses. We were to receive further orders in Ottawa telling us where our next posting would take us, and when.

Several of us were approached and offered jobs as civilian instructors for a new "mystery" class due in the following week. I declined. The RAF had gotten me this far and I felt obligated to stick around a while despite the very attractive salary offered; $400 per month. A few remained behind, and I often wondered how they got on with the new group as I read a few months later that Jacqueline Cochran had started a class at Sweetwater for an all female group of ferry pilots, known as WASPS. These lads were to be their instructors. I should add, I never heard from any of them again. They were a randy bunch and may not have survived!

I spent a few days at home, then took off for Ottawa and checked into one of the finest hotels in the city – The Chateau St. Laurent. I couldn't have made a better choice. It was filled with flying types, some in civvies but most in uniform. In the bar, I learned that the ones in civvies were ferry pilots responsible for delivering Mosquito fighter-bombers that had been manufactured in Canada, to various points in the United Kingdom (UK). These were the latest design by deHavilland. Constructed of moulded plywood with twin Rolls Royce Merlins, they were faster than most fighters of their time.

The young man in charge of the group had learned that I had been trained under the British scheme in the States and was still a civilian. He offered me a chance to join them, saying I would be expected to take a two-week familiarization course at Dorval, Canada, all expenses paid. Each pilot was entitled to at least one trip a month, more if he wished, starting as co-pilot ("second Dickey") for two trips at $1,000 per trip and then moving up to Chief pilot ("first Dickey") at $1,500 per trip. I spent a long, restless night pondering that one before deciding to refuse, with the same reasoning as before: the RAF had gotten me this far, etc.

The next morning I checked in with the proper authorities and was given identification papers and instructions to report to No. 31 Personnel Depot (PD), Moncton, New Brunswick, Canada.

8. Moncton

Moncton was a holding station for RAF personnel awaiting repatriation and Canadian aircrew headed for England. This place was a crowded madhouse of "organized disorganization." It was as cold as hell, the food was terrible, and with everyone else in uniform, I felt badly out of place. None of my class had arrived but I supposed, wrongly, that they would be along later. As if all this wasn't bad enough, I woke up one dark night on my hands and knees just outside the emergency room, never knowing how I got there.

Unable to stand and with terrible pains in my chest, I was helped by a kind passer-by into the infirmary, where they tucked me into a nice warm bed, and I passed out. Up to that point in my life I had never heard of pleurisy, but that was the diagnosis and it meant at least ten days to two weeks in bed. My feet were not to touch the floor, even to go to the bathroom.

I had one roommate, Sydney Brown, an Australian; a nice chap who had been badly burned in a flying accident. He had been there for two months when he contracted pleurisy and was placed with me in isolation. Our nurse was a Newfoundlander, Jean Clary, perhaps only a bit older than we, but she took care of us as though we were her own children. Syd taught me to play cribbage (at my expense). I'll never forget "…and one for his knob," as I lost another game.

Things were rather dull until one night I happened to be lying facing the window half asleep. When I opened my eyes, I felt as though I had received an electric shock. It was completely black outside except for a shimmering rainbow of luminescent colours fanning from horizon to horizon and flashing to directly over-head. I honestly thought I had died. Reality returned when I heard Sydney say, "There's that bloody *aurora borealis* again." Having never seen it before, I found it a frightening but gorgeous sight.

In ten days I had mended to such a degree, I was told I was entitled to two weeks' sick leave. I felt that one would be sufficient and the next day was on the way to Richmond. But with most of my friends gone and little to do, I was eager to leave when it came time to return. It was a lonely trip back, with an overnight layover in New York. I spent most of the evening, alone, in the lounge of the Statler Hotel, listening to the Jimmy Dorsey orchestra, with Helen O'Connell singing "Green Eyes," and enjoying a few beers.

On my return, the Adjutant suggested that since England had such a severe shortage of clothing, I might be wise to buy my dress uniform, cap and greatcoat locally, which I did. They lasted for the entire length of my service, almost five years, and hang in my closet today.

Mother loved Wedgewood china and I had bought her a dozen beautiful serving plates in one of the shops in Moncton. I was telling one of the chaps in the mess hall that I had hoped to get them to Richmond without paying the duty tax. A Royal Canadian Air Force (RCAF) Flight Lieutenant overheard the conversation and volunteered to take the package to Washington DC when he flew down the next day to see his fiancée. Eighteen months later while in North Africa, I had a letter from Mother telling me it had just arrived with a note from the Flight Lieutenant. Apparently he had been badly hurt in a crash landing in Canada on the way down. When he was leaving the hospital a year later, they gave him his belongings salvaged from the wreckage, and among them was the package of china. Not a single plate was chipped or broken. He mailed them, and in his note to Mother, he even apologized for the delay in delivery! But Dad still had to pay the duty…

There was a very interesting group around the bar at night. Most of the RAF types had big smiles, knowing they would soon be on the boat for "Old Blighty." Some had been away for several years. The RCAF lads didn't share their joy, having been told that most of them would probably be gone 'for the duration' and realizing that, for some, this might mean forever.

I'm forced to confess I was looking forward to leaving: first, because I would soon be flying aircraft I had never seen before; second, I had never been abroad; and third, having heard from some of the RAF chaps the terrible problems they were facing (bombings, rationing, shortages of almost everything and the possibility of invasion) I couldn't help wanting to see for myself.

The pool of humanity at Moncton was changing so rapidly that there wasn't a chance to really get to know one another. Pilot Officer Peter Wyagle had been away from home for two years training at an RAF flight school in Alabama, and was the only Englishman I met who really hated to leave. He had fallen in love with a girl who lived in a small town near where he had been stationed, and he would talk to me for hours late into the evenings describing their courtship in lurid detail. Some of their escapades were quite hilarious, but most wouldn't bear repeating here.

We became good friends and fortunately, when the time came, we were posted together. His instructions to me were invaluable. I knew nothing about British military protocol, how they marched, the names of the ranks of their officers and airmen, how to salute, nor did I understand British currency – pounds, shillings and pence were particularly puzzling. Our marching and saluting practice sessions took place behind one of the old buildings. He, acting as the Sergeant Major drill master and I, as the raw recruit in civvies, we marched up and down: "right turn," "left turn," "about face," "by the left quick march," etc. Anyone watching would have thought we were "bonkers," but it gave us something to do and later proved to be quite useful.

9. HMS Queen Elizabeth

Names were posted on a large bulletin board each day listing those who were scheduled to depart to various parts of the globe, never giving the destination because of security regulations. Only name, rank, serial number, and time to be at the transportation depot were posted. Wyagle came racing into the barracks one morning in a great state of excitement. Both of our names were posted. Sure enough, there it was, "Smith, P. F." – no rank and no number but no doubt that I was included.

I thought it strange that none of the others in my class had shown up, and I learned later that I was the last American lucky enough to be "exported" to the RAF. The others had wandered off to better paying jobs as civilian instructors or whatever. This included my old roommate, Fred Hill, whom I have seen several times since the war, the last on his 50th wedding anniversary in 1998.

We rushed to get packed and were waiting at the station with about fifty other souls for at least an hour before departure time, everyone with his RAF kit bag, identifiable by a horizontal blue stripe and the owner's name, rank and serial number. I, wearing a tweed sports jacket and carrying a leather valise, stuck out like a sore thumb.

Wyagle managed to scrounge two seats together in one of Canadian National's newest cars. We propped up our feet, lit cigarettes, and began to speculate on our destination. It most certainly had to be a seaport on the East Coast, and while we had no idea of the size of the ship we might be on, we guessed the port would be Halifax, Boston or New York. As the day wore on, we passed Halifax and that left Boston or New York. Boston went by in the dark (the whole East Coast was under blackout regulations,) and we continued going at a pretty good clip. Hours later we felt the train slowing and we were then certain it was New York. When it finally stopped, there was a mad rush to disembark.

We stepped off into pouring rain, and pitch black darkness lit only by waving, shielded flashlights. With all the shouting of instructions and questions and noise of machinery, it was bedlam. I could barely make out the huge steel side of a ship, a gangplank that rose up to a dimly lit doorway, and a continuous stream of humanity climbing up and into the hull. A uniformed officer stood at the bottom handing out berthing cards which indicated the deck, stateroom, and number of one's bunk as well as the times of meals and location of each dining room table. There would be two meals a day.

Lugging my suitcase, I struggled up the gangplank to the doorway and stepped into a brilliantly lit lobby. On the wall was a huge, beautiful British cartouche with the ship's name – HMS *Queen Elizabeth*. When Wyagle compared our cards, we were disappointed to note that they were in no way similar, but we agreed to meet later, shook hands, and went our separate ways. It was four days before we met again.

The long smoky corridor leading out of the lobby was teeming with humanity shuffling along "cheek to cheek and jowl to jowl." Judging from my berthing card, my bunk would be one deck below, so I eased my way over and down the next stairway and was swept along to the doorway of my cabin. I slipped out of the stream, and stepped inside.

What was once a double stateroom was now filled with five rows of bunks, four bunks high, with so little clearance between them that a medium sized man would have trouble turning over.

I found the one with my number, and noted it was filled with a kit bag and other personal belongings, as well as a rather large Flight Sergeant. I suggested as tactfully as possible that he might be in my assigned bunk, and asked him to compare his card with mine. He did, and the deck number, cabin number and bunk number were identical. I looked around and realized that nothing could be worse than this, so I told him to remain where he was, and I would go in search of the purser.

I dragged my suitcase up one deck and along to what appeared to be a lobby. There it was, "Purser's Office," and it seemed to be occupied. Rather than risk the possibility of being thrown ashore because of lack of space, I decided to wait until we were under way, and then seek his help. With my rather indefinite military status in mind, I wondered as I sat outside the purser's office, if I really was supposed to be on board or if that berthing card had been rigged. If it was not intentional, it was indeed a strange coincidence.

I waited for an hour or more until I felt the vibration of the engines and the ship moving before I dared to face the purser. It was past midnight after a long day, and yet he listened patiently to my story. He couldn't have been more sympathetic. He asked that I wait a little longer in the corridor until everyone had settled down, and in the meanwhile, he would look over the passenger list and see what, if any, accommodations might still be available.

Things were much calmer when he reappeared with torch (flashlight) in hand and indicated I was to follow him two flights up to another corridor. This one was almost empty except for a few of the crew. He stopped at a stateroom door, opened it quietly, and with the aid of his torch, guided me across the totally darkened room to the upper of a double bunk. With a whispered, "Cheers," he left me standing there. Trying not to disturb the fellow in the lower bunk, I eased myself up, stretched out fully clothed, and fell into a deep sleep.

I awoke with a start, staring into a brilliant ceiling light, with someone shaking me, suggesting that I "wakey, wakey." (Oh how many times I was to hear that wake-up call in the years to come!) The hand doing the shaking protruded from a blue dress uniform sleeve showing one broad ring about two inches wide, denoting the rank of a very senior officer. Its owner introduced himself as Air Commodore (A/C) Foster.

Seeing me dressed as I was, I am certain he thought I was some sort of governmental official or spy or mad scientist, and it didn't help much when I told him my name was "Smith." He told me he and the other room occupants were leaving for breakfast and the bathroom was all mine. I could hardly believe it: there were only five of us in this huge, luxury suite, the A/C, a Group Captain, two Squadron Leaders, and me. The sixth bunk was unoccupied. I dug into my case for my shaving kit, toothbrush, etc., and headed for the bath, thinking about those less fortunate beggars that were crowded twenty to a bathroom much smaller than this. Ah, such is life.

Having performed my ablutions, I dressed and headed to the officers' dining room in accordance with my boarding card, which read, "Officers' Dining Room, R Deck Aft, Table 47, Second Sitting, Breakfast 9:30 ~ Dinner 7:00." Once again the smoky corridors were filled with humanity, mostly "Yanks," shuffling along to nowhere. I noticed that one minute it felt as though we were walking up an incline, and twenty seconds later, running down a hill. This was due to the pitching of the ship, its 1100-foot length, and the absence of any natural horizon. The stairway walls were decorated with beautiful murals, which were mostly hidden under large, protective, plywood panels. Our dining room had once been a huge swimming pool that was now covered with temporary flooring.

The tables were set with "HMS Queen Elizabeth" inscribed "silver," beautiful china, linen tablecloths, and *flowers* in the centre. The décor would have rivalled that of the renowned Stork Club in New York. Uniformed waiters were scurrying about with eighteen-inch menus listing juices, fruits, steaks, English, American and Canadian sausages, eggs in any form, kippers, bacon, freshly baked bread, rolls, real butter, apple pie, and believe it or not, ice cream!

The returning English, the Canadians and I, who had been stuck in one of the personnel depots with their awful food, were stunned by the waiter's suggestion that we try several entrees - there was no limit! Dinner at night was just as lavish. There were big, thick slices of roast beef, salmon, duckling, every type of salad ever concocted, milk, tea, coffee, cake, ice cream again, pies, etc – all one could eat. It's hard to imagine how they were able to supply, prepare and serve the 18,000 souls on board with 36,000 such lavish meals every day for three and a half days in the midst of a war. I was told, this was the largest number passengers ever carried by HMS Queen Elizabeth.

Following breakfast, I went in search of the officer's lounge, hoping to catch up with Wyagle. I found it located on one of the higher decks. It was as large as a football field, and even without furniture, there was "standing room only."

Men and a very few women were packed in like sardines. It reminded me of some of the New Year's Eve parties at the Country Club at home, with almost everyone smoking and talking at the same time, nowhere to sit, and jammed in so close together that if one had fainted, he would never have hit the floor.

I didn't see Wyagle, but I heard a familiar voice behind me, and turned to discover an old Richmond neighbour, Dr. Thomas

Murrell. We had a nice but brief visit, and on parting, promised to look each other up later that evening. However, we failed to give each other our stateroom locations. I didn't see him again until we were back in Richmond in 1946, four years later.

We were allowed on the open deck, and could smoke in daytime but never at night. I went out to take a look after breakfast the first morning, and was amazed to see what appeared to be two destroyers on our port side, straining to keep up and looking like greyhounds just let out of the kennel. They were there only throughout that morning, until we were clear of the German submarine packs that prowled the coast. Then they dropped astern as we increased to a speed that exceeded their ability to keep abreast. As soon as they were out of sight, we began a zigzag pattern to, hopefully, avoid any enemy vessel that might by lying in wait. As we were the fastest thing afloat, they would have only one chance for a lucky shot. They could never catch up with us.

The open decks were crowded, and those out next to the rail were busily carving their names or initials which, I understand, remain to this day. I returned to the cabin and found my roommates all there, preferring its quiet comfort to the madhouse outside. They were obviously curious about me, and began asking "how, what, when and where." I had to admit that I was a civilian with no idea when I was supposed to don the uniform of a Pilot Officer. They asked to see my travel vouchers, which I produced. The A/C studied them carefully and said that since they were written for "Pilot Officer Smith" and as we were past the three-mile continental limit, I should dress accordingly, and not worry about taking the "King's oath" until we reached RAF headquarters in London.

Due to the crowded conditions throughout the ship, we all spent most of our time in the stateroom. There were signs everywhere stating there was to be no smoking in the rooms. If one wanted to smoke, he or she had to go on deck or use the main lounge. The A/C paid little attention however, and was constantly lighting up. We were sitting there talking at about ten o'clock in the morning the second day out, when the door burst open and an American MP stood there, pad and pencil in hand, poised to write the names of any offenders. The A/C, caught red-handed, had his name placed on the list, and was told to report to the Captain immediately. When he hadn't returned after several hours, we were concerned that he might be in the brig. At noon he finally showed up with a big smile on his face, and was immediately peppered with questions. He and the Captain had spent two hours rehashing earlier war experiences. When it came time to leave, the Skipper said he had been told about the A/C's "most serious infraction of the smoking rule," but as the A/C was his superior in rank, there was little he could do other than suggest the A/C "tick himself off severely," and request that he please refrain from smoking whilst in the cabin.

The ship's Tannoy (public address system) was always so busy with instructions, pages and other announcements that one scarcely paid attention to its constant chatter. However, on the third day out, "Stand by for disembarkation instructions," was heard. Immediately, there was complete silence as everyone stopped what he was doing and waited for the rest of the announcement.

We were to be packed and ready to leave the ship the next morning at 2 am. It didn't take long to prepare. We gathered up our things, stuffed them into our kit bags or suitcases, and were sitting on our bunks long before dinner that night, speculating on where we were to land and how. At 1:30 am we were told to descend to one of the lower decks, keeping with our cabin mates. At exactly 2:00 we joined the mass of personnel shuffling down the stairways, headed for the specified deck, all the while trying to stay together. I was more than anxious not to be separated from the rest.

We reached the bottom of the stairway, and were confronted with an enormous cargo door which opened out to pouring rain, and a night as black as the inside of a derby hat. A gangplank led down to what we found to be a large, open barge, and as we squeezed on board, still hanging together, a voice with a heavy Scottish accent rang out, "Welcome to Greenock, Mates." This, then, had to be Scotland.

We were in the Firth of Clyde. Nearby would be Glasgow and, hopefully, shelter from the freezing, teeming rain. We were led by flashlight to a roofless railway station. However, the station was not far from where we were "debarged," and a train was waiting. With the A/C in the lead, a first-class compartment for six was located. Having never been on an English train, I was pleasantly surprised. It was neat and clean and the seats, though worn, were comfortable. We were well under way before we discovered that there were no lights and no heat, and as the train gathered speed, the icy air began to infiltrate the compartment. Our soaking wet greatcoats only increased our discomfort.

Having heard there was a shortage of Scotch in England, I had purchased six pints before leaving Canada, which were packed in the bottom of my case. I casually asked if anyone cared for a drink and the response was overwhelming. One of the pints was well on the way to extinction when a Squadron Leader headed off to the "loo." He reappeared a few moments later to announce his discovery of a compartment right next to ours that was filled with American Red Cross girls! He suggested that since I was an American, it was my duty to invite them to join our group of "glamorous" RAF pilots for a little libation. This was to be the first command given me as an officer in the Royal Air Force, "Go get the girls," and it gave rise to the thought that this might be a very interesting war!

The Squadron Leader was correct. The next compartment *was* filled with young ladies, all just as cold and wet as we were. After I had introduced myself and told them I was from Virginia, I asked if they would be interested in joining our group next door for cocktails. The reply was immediate, in the affirmative, and very enthusiastic. There were eight of them and when they joined the six of us, the compartment, having only six seats, seemed a bit crowded. Someone had produced a torch which produced enough light, when combined with the constant flare of matches, and glow of cigarettes, to enable one to dimly make out the person he or she was talking to.

Out came several bottles of the remaining whiskey, which were passed hand to hand, everyone taking a sip as one went by. Introductions were made (I learned that one of the girls was from Richmond), and the party began. I had always heard that the British were reserved, but it wasn't long before any initial shyness was overcome. The suggestion was made that we all try to sit down, and since there were only six seats for fourteen people, there would have to be a little "lap dancing."

Although still wearing our greatcoats, we were wet and chilled to the bone. Someone mentioned that huddling together to create a little warmth might be a good idea. Oh how true, how true! It wasn't long before the arm rests were making things uncomfortable and the floor seemed a better place to settle, provided that everyone would join in. There was very little argument on that score, and within minutes the whole crowd became a squirming pile of bodies on the carpeted floor. In the dim light it was difficult to tell who was who, but it only took a few giggles and ribald comments to clear that problem.

Eventually, things quieted down. Being as heavily dressed as we were, I was quite sure nothing "unseemly" was taking place. Most of us, full of grog, drifted off to sleep. I remembered that some of these officers were married or engaged, and were probably going to be met at the station upon our arrival in London. We pulled into Euston Station at about 6 am and the scramble began. The thoroughly hung over group exchanged a few hugs and kisses and the usual pleasantries and then tried to make themselves presentable to the public.

Bleary-eyed, unshaven, hair amuss and teeth unbrushed, we were a sorry sight. The Red Cross girls exited first, and were immediately formed into ranks standing at ease. A near crisis arose when the wife of the Group Captain, who had been abroad for a year, rushed into his arms, only to hear as they passed by the girls, "Thanks, Groupie. Last night was wonderful!" Then I heard, "Dear, was that young girl speaking to you?"

Euston Station, like most of the London rail stations, was at least two city blocks long with a hundred-foot ceiling that had formerly been covered with panes of glass. These had been intentionally removed for pedestrian safety or blown out by bomb explosions. Only the soot-stained steel framework remained. It was still raining quite hard and with no roof, one might just as well have been standing in an open field. We were soaked again.

I demonstrated my newly learned salute to my cabin mates as we told each other good bye, dragged my heavy suitcase to the nearest exit and hailed one of the ever-present London cabs. They seemed to be everywhere. Some, I noticed, due to the fuel shortage, were operated by gas vapour, carried on the roof in a bag that looked like an enormous vacuum cleaner. I gave my driver the address of the Adastral House in Whitehall, RAF headquarters, and sat back to view the almost complete ruin of what had once been a perfectly beautiful city.

Block after block had been levelled and the few buildings not totally destroyed were mostly hollow shells, standing ghostlike, with vacant windows and doorways – roofless, dirty, smoke-stained and depressing in the early morning rain and fog. The cold, miserable weather demanded that everyone light up his precious coal fire, and the resulting sooty smoke from thousands of chimney pots added to the misty gloom. Visibility at times was no more than a few yards.

I arrived at headquarters and presented the Adjutant with the papers given me when I left Canada. I was immediately ushered into an office occupied by a kindly-looking, elderly Group Captain, whose batman had just arrived with morning tea. He invited me to be seated and join him in taking tea. Having not eaten since we left the ship the previous evening, I was famished and quickly accepted. The scones, little watercress sandwiches and bits of sardines on biscuits were practically tasteless compared to the shipboard fare, but with very little help from the Group Captain they disappeared in a hurry.

He asked me questions about my flying background and the type of operations I preferred. I told him my flying experience was all listed in my log book, which was to have been sent over months ago. There was no record of it having been received and it remains missing to this day. My only identification papers were my travel warrants and a copy of my birth certificate.

He listened to my description of my background and training and must have thought no one would be stupid enough to go to such trouble as to fake all of that.

Was it my honest face, or they really being so desperate for pilots, that made him quickly decide that I should be sent to Harrogate, a holding station for further posting to an Advanced

Flying Unit (AFU), where they could judge my ability? There was no time for the usual initial flight instruction. If I passed, I would proceed with training as an operational pilot. If not, it would be back to the States.

It is hard to imagine something such as this taking place in the American forces, yet with the British, it was to happen time and time again that "red tape" was cut in my favour. He asked that I stand at attention and repeat after him an oath swearing my allegiance to the King, which I did. In so doing I gained my commission as a Pilot Officer (acting) and serial number 134347, and in the process, lost my citizenship in the USA. (Two years later, my citizenship was restored by an act of Congress applying to all Americans who had taken an oath to the King in order to serve in the British forces.)

10. Wartime London

I wandered around London for the rest of the day, trying to absorb the massive destruction done by the relentless, almost continuous, day and night bombing. The buildings left standing were covered with dust and grime and blackened with smoke from the fire storms caused by phosphorous incendiaries. In some instances, whole blocks had disappeared, leaving gaping foundations filled with rubble. The sky was filled with tethered, sausage-like antiaircraft balloons with dangling wires, all dancing in the stiff breezes.

Massive, fifty-foot, open-topped steel tanks filled with water for fire fighting were on every corner, and sandbags filled the entrance doorways and first storey windows of the buildings that still remained standing. The beautiful wrought-iron fences that had surrounded the apartments or flats, private homes and parks had been taken as scrap and melted down for munitions.

There were temporary bomb shelters every few hundred yards at street level and the underground tube stations and platforms were turned into overnight shelters, crowded with bunks, cots and sleeping mats. Almost everyone, man or woman, over the age of fifty and not eligible for the services, was enlisted as an air raid warden, fire warden or marshal, destined to spend long days and nights patrolling the streets and rooftops, watching for enemy aircraft and fires resulting from the raids.

Everywhere there were huge bomb craters. Some, smaller than others, were surrounded by police barriers and terrifying posters warning "UXB" – an unexploded bomb awaiting the attention of some of the bravest of all, those heroes who volunteered to descend into the crater and disarm the monster before it did its work. There were several hundred courageous souls who specialized in this work and information released after the war, revealed that this was the most hazardous war duty of any in the British Empire.

There was very little motorized traffic in the city apart from the taxis and the rush hour was made up of thousands of cyclists. Everyone, young or old, rich or poor, rode a bicycle. They followed the rules of the road, driving on the left and stopping for traffic lights as well as the pedestrian crosswalks. Most of the very dignified looking, usually elderly gentlemen and lady cyclists were properly dressed for office work or shopping, umbrellas on the crossbar, mackintoshes in the basket, the men with clips on the cuffs of their trousers.

Each carried or wore a tin helmet and had a gas mask slung over his or her shoulder as required by law. Some of the shops were open, with such windows as remained, taped or covered with plywood to help protect from flying glass.

I had been given a "chit," good for a room and a meal at one of the hotels and I decided it was time to eat and try to get some rest. I chose the Regent Palace off Piccadilly Circus, where, although the bar was crowded, there seemed to be plenty of accommodations. The rooms were large and dreary and the bath and toilets were at the end of the hall. All bathtubs had a line painted around them four inches from the bottom, and a sign was posted on the wall reminding everyone that it was against the law to fill the tub with hot water any higher than the line. This was obeyed by everyone; I'm sure; certainly by me. A large ceramic, open-topped tank was suspended about seven feet above the toilet with a length of chain hanging within reach of the user. When one pulled the chain to flush, a good portion of the water cascaded over the top, to the dismay of anyone who failed to stand far enough aside. (This was standard equipment throughout the country's pubs, wherever there was inside plumbing.)

My sleep was interrupted several times by the explosion of bombs and antiaircraft fire. Sirens, bells and whistles of fire and rescue vehicles sounded constantly. I couldn't resist drawing back the blackout curtains to get a look at an air raid. The sky was aglow to the east with occasional flames leaping up over the smoke-filled horizon, outlining the houses and taller buildings. The raid was over as quickly as it started, but the area was smouldering long after daybreak.

There was an "American Eagle Club" in the centre of London, established for the benefit of those Americans connected with the RAF. I found it located on Charing Cross Road, and run by a wonderful ex-American lady, Mrs. Francis Dexter. She informed me that we could use the club to sleep, eat and receive mail, which they would forward to wherever we might happen to be. This was a great convenience. I had an address from which letters would be forwarded to the different stations in England, as well as those in North Africa, Italy, and Scotland. (Some took as long as six months but most did, finally, arrive. One or two were so charred by fire that they were difficult to read.)

Mrs. Dexter allowed me to store my civilian clothes and my big, heavy leather suitcase, which was replaced by the regulation canvas kit bag, making life a lot easier. She and I remained friends and corresponded for many years after the war.

I arrived in Harrogate by train, and was depressed to see an ancient group of smoke-stained buildings, once a university campus, that had been turned into a "holding pen" for unruly officer personnel. Thank heaven, I was billeted in a section reserved for transients.

There was a problem in disciplining officers for breeches of regulations not severe enough to require incarceration in what was known as "The Glass House" – the air force jail. Being out of uniform, improperly dressed, fraternizing with the ranks, general unpleasant attitude, drunkenness, etc., were all causes for reduction in rank and time at Harrogate. The officers there were constantly harassed by being made to change from sports clothing to full dress uniform and back again every hour from five in the morning until eight at night. Failure to follow these instructions, usually given by a Flight Sergeant, resulted in being ""cashiered"," a dishonourable discharge that ruined one for life.

The day after arrival, I was summoned to the office of the Wing Commander in charge of postings to operational training units (OTUs) for Bomber or Fighter Command. He was very abrupt and didn't seem at all interested in my previous training. He informed me that they needed bomber pilots and I was to be posted to a multi-engine OTU. I tried to make him aware that all my training up to this point had been on single-engine aircraft, but it didn't seem to alter his position and he began writing up my posting.

At home in Richmond I had a Boston bulldog of a rare breed known as the "Haggerty Strain." To my amazement, on the W/C's desk was a photograph of the same type of dog. While he was writing, I reached for my wallet and pulled out a picture of Mother and "Nod" and held it up to his photograph. That did it. He pushed all the papers aside and for the next half hour we talked about our dogs. He was all smiles, and by now, instead of Pilot Officer Smith, I had become just "Smithy."

"You are obviously not interested in Bomber Command, just what posting would you like?"

"Fighter Command," I replied.

He thought for a moment and then asked, "How about Tern Hill for preparation for Spitfires, Hurricanes, and Mustangs?"

I couldn't believe it! I accepted, and the posting was written. He handed me the papers, and I did my best to keep from smiling as I thanked him and saluted, thinking how often one's life hinges on such small things as a photograph.

I also took note of "Smithy" – not the usual "Smitty," but "Smithy." It was to be my nickname throughout my entire association with the RAF.

Mother and 'Nod'.

11.   No. 5 AFU ~ Tern Hill

Tern Hill was an advanced flying unit (AFU), employed to check one's ability to fly larger and more powerful aircraft. It was a permanent station located among the rolling hills of Shropshire in central England, and probably one of the most beautiful in the RAF, even during wartime.

The train conductor announced the station, and as I retrieved my kit bag from the baggage car I noticed it had been carefully slit and several cartons of cigarettes had been removed.

Alone, I stepped off onto the small platform of an ivy-covered brick railway station, deserted except for a few pigeons. The soft hissing of the little steam engine faded as it departed, leaving me in complete silence. Had it not been announced, I wouldn't have had any idea where I was. All railroad signs throughout the country had been removed, as had road, town and hamlet identifications, in order to confuse any attempt of invasion by the enemy.

As I stood there, I heard for the first time the never-to-be-forgotten, soft, soothing, sigh-like whistle of a Spitfire with its Merlin engine as it turned on an approach to a runway hidden from my sight by the steep railroad embankment. Then I heard what was to become another familiar sound – the characteristic "popping" noise from the exhaust stacks as the throttle was fully retarded for landing.

A dream was about to be fulfilled. After months of uncertainty, my future as a pilot in the Royal Air Force lay just over that railroad embankment, and I could hardly wait! Unless I put up a terrible "black," I would shortly be flying a Hurricane or Spitfire!

A wizened old chap stuck his head out of the doorway and said, "Sir, if you are needing transport to the station, I'll ring them up for a van." Within fifteen minutes it appeared, driven by a smartly-uniformed WAAF (Women's Auxiliary Air Force) Corporal. I was saluted and addressed as "Pilot Officer Smith." "Sir," she said, "I am Corporal Joyce Gill, your driver." Before I could protest, she had lifted my kit bag and greatcoat into the back and was standing by the door on the passenger side – the left side. She could tell by the USA "flash" (emblem) on my shoulder that I was a Yank and tried to suppress a smile as I made an attempt to climb in on the right side, the wrong side in England.

Very little was said during the ten-minute ride to the aerodrome, but this later changed, and she became a regular chatterbox after we got to know each other. Joyce was a big help. As the station switchboard operator, she knew almost everyone, and seemed to take a special interest in introducing me to the others and steering me around the enormous mess.

We drew up in front of a large, beautiful Georgian building with pigeons and rooks lining the roof ridge. It had all the appearance of a very wealthy family's estate. Located on top of a hill, the building would disappear in low clouds. The rooks, being smarter than most of us, would perch on the roof and wait for it to clear, while flight training carried on as usual on the aerodrome below.

A batman scurried out and took my things and then led me some distance away to a room in a "Nissen hut," a structure not unlike a Quonset hut, where I was turned over to my batwoman. Let me try to explain, lest this be misunderstood.

Every officer was entitled to a servant, or "batman." These fine young, or in some cases elderly, enlisted, non-commissioned airmen and airwomen were indispensable. They usually took care of two or three officers each. They shined shoes and buttons, pressed uniforms, took care of laundry, stoked fires (three lumps of coal in the morning and three at night), brought morning tea when awakening their officers and performed hundreds of other housekeeping chores that others might consider demeaning, but not these hard-working people. They were up before the sun on bone-chilling mornings for a fourteen to sixteen-hour day and sometimes with little or no sleep due to the air raids. They put heart and soul into their work. There was a war on and they, with few exceptions, were determined to do their part. Their pride was reflected in the appearance of "their officer."

This system remained in effect even when one was outside the UK. Overseas, where there wasn't sufficient manpower available, each officer received a "hard living allowance," a few extra shillings a day, in order to hire a civilian to perform these same duties. There was reasoning in all this. It was for morale and discipline. An officer was expected to be properly attired and well-dressed, and this would be almost impossible with flying and classes occupying most of his waking hours. The system did produce a few prima-donnas who took advantage, but they were soon recognized, and dealt with by the batmen in one of the many subtle ways a disgruntled servant can invent.

One example was in the laundry. To my surprise, many Englishmen didn't wear underpants. Instead, the regulation shirts were made (by Van Heusen) with unusually long shirttails, which were drawn up between the legs. One snotty officer, known by all for complaining about the condition of his shirts, pinned a note on his shirttail, "Not so much damned *starch,* please." It was returned the next day with a note on the shirttail, "Not so much damned *brown*, please." He tried for days to file disciplinary charges against the laundress but no one would tell him who she was.

My batwoman was WAAF Leading Aircraftswoman (LACW) Rose Canfield (never called "Rose", always "Canfield.") She was as new to the service as I, but well trained and always cheerful and eager to please. Without being asked, she very quickly unpacked my kit bag, put things away and was polishing buttons and pressing the trousers of my dress blues within minutes of my arrival. I again made the hasty, and faulty, judgment that this was going to be a beautiful war.

All officers were expected to have a greatcoat, a mackintosh, a dress uniform, battle-dress, a peaked cap and a forage cap, blue shirts with stiff collars, a black tie and black dress shoes as well as brown dress gloves. I had bought all of this in Canada except the shoes. Mine were brown to go with my civvies, and up to the time I arrived at Tern Hill, I had been wearing black galoshes under my trousers, intending to buy black shoes when I got to a shoemaker with the necessary ration coupons. As I have said, Tern Hill was a permanent training station. Training stations were notorious for "spit and polish" (also known as "bullshit") as they were usually staffed with elderly "Regular Service" who stuck to the old traditions they were used to. Nothing wrong with that, but most of the flying types were "Volunteer Reserves" who wore the insignia "VR" on their uniform collars and knew very little about old traditions, among which were the "Mess Regulations." One never *ever* wore any type of flying clothing when in the mess and one never discussed politics, religion or women. Imagine!

Canfield suggested that I hurry along to tea before it was all gone. I arrived in the enormous anteroom where tea was being served. And that was about all it was, little tasteless crumpets and small watercress finger sandwiches and, of course, tea. I was starved but got one or two before they were all gone. All of us were hungry, and were to stay that way for the next four years, until the war was over.

Standing there, I was approached by a Flight Lieutenant who introduced himself as the "mess secretary." My first thought was, "What a nice fellow; he wants to make me feel at home." Instead, he asked me to leave at once as I was improperly dressed. Then he turned and walked away. Not having any idea what the hell he was talking about and feeling that everyone was staring at me, I returned to the safety of the Nissen hut and Canfield for an explanation.

She was horrified to see she had let her officer go out improperly dressed! It was my galoshes. They had been taken for flying clothing. She was most apologetic, took my shoes into her little workroom, and in a few minutes returned with the blackest ex-brown shoes I had ever seen. She had dyed them on the spot!

While this was taking place, I got a lesson in the difference between the "King's" English and American English. Many expressions were to plague me for at least a year. I had left my sewing kit (which they called a "housewife") on the bed, and as Canfield stood there with my shoes, I sat to put them on, landing on one of the sewing needles. I muttered an oath and said something about sticking a needle in my "fanny." She turned beet red and rushed out of the room. It was hours before I could get her to speak to me. It took even more time for her to come around to explaining that in England the word "fanny" referred to a girl's most private parts. The proper term for one's rear was "bum." Now this meant that I could no longer properly refer to someone as "a bum!"

Another bit of confusion: In the middle of a long-distance phone call, the operator would break in and ask, "Are you through? Are you through?" Meaning, "Have you gotten your connection?" You answer, "No! No!" Meaning, "I have not finished talking." She would then say, "Sorry, we'll try again" and break the connection. This might occur several times before I realized what the problem was.

Now being properly dressed, I returned to the mess as it was getting on toward what I hoped would be supper time, only to hear announced over the Tannoy for all to hear, "Pilot Officer Smith 134347 is to report to the Adjutant's office at 0830 tomorrow in best blues." This could only mean one thing; I was going to get a "rocket."

Trying to pretend that I had no idea who this fellow "Smith" was, I strolled around the anteroom. There were at least fifty bodies, student pilots as well as instructors, in a fog of cigarette smoke, drinking beer, gin, whiskey and, a new one on me, "lemon squash," all delivered by several mess servants from a well-stocked bar.

Although the conversation was loud and animated, it didn't seem to disturb those playing, what was to become almost a nightly tradition, "Monopoly." I watched for a few minutes, at a complete loss to understand how they were managing since the players were of so many different nationalities. There were French, Turks (they weren't even in the war,) Poles, Hollanders, Norwegians, Canadians, "Aussies," New Zealanders, and many others from around the British Empire. Yet, there was some measure of communication, for although it sounded like the Tower of Babel, the games kept going without interruption.

A piano and two snooker tables were in an adjoining room. Snooker was the British version of pool, pretty much the same as the American version except the pockets were smaller. All permanent stations had at least one table, and the game itself, believe it or not, was a great help in improving deflection shooting. I never saw it used for gambling except for an "arf pint" or so.

Dinner was announced and we all filed into the dining hall. What a shock! This two-story room had a thirty-foot ceiling and a banquet table that seated no less than a hundred people. Again, not knowing the form, I observed very closely. All of the officers were standing behind one of the high-backed chairs and a dozen or so WAAF mess attendants were lined up along the walls. I stood behind a chair and waited, watched, and wondered.

There was silence. A door at the far end opened, and the station Group Captain, with his second in command in tow, entered and strode to the head of the table. The station "Padre" said a short prayer, then "God save the King" was intoned. The Adjutant announced, "Gentlemen, be seated," there was a great scraping of chairs, and the hubbub of conversation began again.

To my absolute astonishment, a four-piece orchestra, seated in an alcove up on what would have been the second floor, began playing the Warsaw Concerto! Here we were, in the middle of a war, sitting on top of a hill in a beautiful, luxurious manor house that was subject to bombing at any moment (it had taken a hit a few weeks back) and an orchestra was playing on the balcony!

The senior officers and instructors were seated at the head of the table and we students at the bottom. Next to me was a Welshman, Vernon "Taffy" Lewis, who later became one of my closest friends. Vern was a good-looking chap with coal black hair, a big walrus moustache, piercing blue eyes, and a devil-may-care attitude. As one might guess, he was devastating with the ladies. He was married to a beautiful girl, whom I met later. She was just as devastating as he was.

As we sat there waiting to be served, I noticed a few large, hard biscuits (crackers) in a tray beside a small container of mustard. At home, it wasn't unusual for me to lather French's mustard on a cracker for a little snack. I picked one up and Vern looked on with amazement as I, in my ignorance, smeared on a generous dollop of English mustard. With the first bite, I disgraced myself. It was hot, fiery hot! I reached quickly for water to put out the fire and knocked the glass into Vern's lap. He stood up and it crashed to the floor, attracting everyone's attention. The silence could have been cut with a knife. Then there was a round of applause as Vern stood and covered his privates with a serviette and bowed to the head of the table.

Dinner was served and it was awful; consisting of a very small portion of mutton, carrots, and something that I learned later was called "bubble and squeak" (a mixture of baked mashed potatoes and Brussels sprouts). Dessert came and I was asked if I preferred a "sweet" or a "savoury." I chose the sweet, which was fairly good, a strange sort of custard poured over stale cake, and Vern took the savoury, a very small sardine on a strip of toast.

I very quickly learned that all servings were small. Margarine, one patty per meal, as well as jam, was applied directly from its serving dish to the bread or scone so as to not waste even a smidgen. Tea was already sweetened and sugar was rationed to one teaspoon per meal. Eggs were powdered, there was little or no fruit, and the strip of bacon at breakfast must have been sliced with a razor. I was usually able to satisfy my hunger pangs with some of the ever-present best cheddar cheese I ever tasted – on biscuits so hard they had to be softened in tea.

I became addicted to the oatmeal porridge that was always served at breakfast. I could usually fill up on this "Scottish style," (with a small pat of margarine and a little salt.) We Americans were told not to drink milk as it wasn't pasteurized and could cause umbric fever.

We retired to the anteroom and the bar for an "arf pint" of "arf and arf," good old warm English beer, half mild and half bitter.

Vern tried to explain the various expressions, most of which originated in the old Royal Navy. "Browned off, cheesed off, knock up, kite, whizzo, gynormous, airscrew, bang on, duff gen or pukka gen, put on a charge, gone for a Burton, bought the farm, fall off the perch, bought it, had it, bloody, bugger off, screw it," all had a special meaning and were going to be difficult to get used to.

To further illustrate the cause for my verbal confusion, I quote from a delightful little book written by Squadron Leader C. H. Ward-Jackson. (Without his permission, I might add, because I have no idea where he could be at the moment.) The title of his book is, *A Piece of Cake! RAF Slang Made Easy.)*

"When the Royal Flying Corps and the Royal Naval Air Service were merged following the First World War, the earliest members were army and navy officers who brought with them the expressions of the two older services, but in the early 20's the RAF began to coin their own language. Later peace years of service in Iraq, Egypt, India and elsewhere brought into the hangars and cockpits a vocabulary peculiar to the air force. To this was added the slang produced by World War II. A letter from one erk to another might read like this:

> *Dear Mate:*
> *Since you were posted to that other outfit I have been thoroughly cheesed off. We have a new station master who is flat out for gravel crushing. Stiffens you rigid. By the way you'll be sorry to learn that P/O Saunders has gone for a Burton. His Wimpy came back looking like a colander one morning, the second dickey crumped her on the deck and when the blood tub got there, Saunders had bought the farm. That piece of HQ knitting sends you her love and hopes you will soon be back in BC. What price you as a path finder, you old stiffener.*

Translation:

> *Dear Woody:*
> *Since you were posted from this Squadron I have been depressed. We have a new Station Commander who is very keen on marching on the parade ground. Bores you to death. By the way you'll be sorry to hear P/O Saunders was killed. His Wellington came home the other morning badly shot up, the copilot crashed it on the airfield but by the time the ambulance got there Saunders was dead. That sexy little girl in Headquarters sends you her love and hopes you'll soon be back in Bomber Command. What a price we pay with you as a Path Finder, you old sod.*

In the Royal Navy, if things went well, each rating (enlisted man) was entitled to one tot of rum per day. It was administered, with the Skipper's permission, at sunset by a chief petty officer. A queue was formed and each man had his "tot" filled from a large flagon. To prevent them from saving several rations for a later party, each tot was drained immediately under the watchful eye of the chief.

In our mess, after completion of the day's flying duties, some wag would stand at the bar and mimic in a loud voice the Navy Commander giving his permission via the Tannoy, "Up Spirits! And stand fast the Holy Ghost!" Then the party began.

Later in the evening after the beer and spirits had begun to flow, conversation became more animated, and the noise level increased. Someone shouted, "High Cock Alorum!" Vern suggested we move back a bit, and watch. A half dozen of the lads leaned over with hands against the wall, legs spread and jackets off. A second and third row joined by grabbing those ahead around the waist and holding on. It looked a bit like a rugger scrum. One by one, those remaining got a running start from the other side of the room, and leaped up on the scrum as far as they could. This continued noisily until the whole pile collapsed. I couldn't help remembering that I got in trouble for just wearing improper shoes in this "very formal" place!

The next morning Canfield had me up, and dressed in best blues, shoes and buttons shined, in time for my command performance with the Adjutant at 8:30am. A Corporal ushered me into the Station Commander's office. The Group Captain (G/C), Wing Commander (W/C) in charge of flying and the Adjutant (Adj) remained seated while I tried my best British salute, and stood at attention. First they asked about my breach of decorum, wearing flying clothes in the mess. They were slightly taken aback when I explained that I had no black shoes, and no way of acquiring them without clothing ration coupons, so I had been wearing black overshoes.

The G/C told the slightly embarrassed Adjutant to make a note to see that this was taken care of as soon as possible. Greatly relieved, I was waiting to be dismissed when the Wing Commander asked to see my log book. They were astonished to learn that I didn't have one. I tried to explain that the training school in Texas had told me "all would be taken care of" and I assumed it had been misplaced in transit. To this day I'm not sure they believed me. My heart sank when I was dismissed, told only that I would be summoned that afternoon. I was certain I was on the way out.

I was back in the Nissen hut discussing with Canfield the real possibility of being dismissed and wondering how I was going to get home, when a call came over the Tannoy, "Pilot Officer Smith 134347 is to report to Wing Commander Flying immediately." It was a fifteen minute walk (I hadn't been issued a bicycle) and I didn't waste any time.

The Wing Commander said that he and the Group Captain had discussed the matter and agreed that I should be given a flight test, and if I passed, I would be given a new log book, and credited with 182 flying hours. (I have no idea how they came up with that figure – should have been at least 300.) What a relief! Short-lived though when I remembered the test would have to be in a Miles Master, known as the world's fastest trainer; half-again larger than anything I had ever flown!

I thanked him, and the test was arranged for the following morning. I was sent to "stores" with a chit that explained I was to be issued clothing coupons for shoes, shirts, underwear, etc., and a complete set of flying gear, a bicycle, and a parachute. These aerodromes were so large that everyone from the Group Captain to the lowest ranking airman or airwoman had a bicycle put on his or her charge. One got around faster and they kept everyone in splendid physical condition. There were some mix-ups, of course, but with each airman having his own, there was no incentive to pinch someone else's. Occasionally one or two would be left outside the local pub at night, the owners having gotten so "sloshed" they forgot they had one and walked home, but being marked the way they were, "RAF Property - Airmen for the use of only," the publican usually had them returned the next morning.

Flying clothes consisted of the following:
- Helmet and goggles
- Oxygen mask with microphone
- Mae West (flotation jacket)
- Heavy fur-lined Irving jacket
- Fur-lined boots
- Leather gauntlets with silk glove liners

- Quilted full-length underalls
- Heavy white wool turtleneck sweater
- Sidcot

The "Sidcot" was a full-length fire resistant coverall designed by Sydney Cotton, a famous English race driver. It was worn over the underalls and the turtleneck sweater. (Most, if not all, equipment was designed to protect against fire. Some crash survivors were so horribly burned that the RAF as well as the Fleet Air Arm had become paranoid. Aircraft fuel tanks were frequently located in front of the windscreen, just above the pilot's lap and it doesn't take much imagination to visualize the ghastly results when these tanks were punctured by a cannon shell or ruptured in a crash.)

12. The Flight Test

Sergeant Pilot Jack Senior was assigned the task of flying me about the area in a twin engine Anson in order to familiarize me with the traffic pattern. Next morning I was turned over to a Canadian Flight Sergeant, Paul Engineer. We met at "flights" at 8:00am as the morning mists were beginning to clear. The fur-lined clothes were for cold, high altitudes, so I had dressed in battle dress, the turtleneck sweater and flying boots. Though it was chilly, I didn't want to be encumbered with all the other heavier stuff.

F/Sgt Engineer introduced me to the Master Mark I, showing me the procedures for starting and stopping the engine, how the wheels and flaps were operated, proper engine temperatures and throttle settings and, I'm sure, a few other things. He asked if I had any questions. I didn't know enough to ask, so I just prayed this monster would fly like the others.

I climbed in and took a look around the Spartan interior. There were no floors or panels or padding covering the wires and plumbing, and no relief tube. One just "went" in the bottom. I often felt British aircraft were built with performance in mind, and the pilot just stuffed in, while the Americans built theirs around the pilot.

The engine and prop controls appeared to be pretty standard. The rudder pedals had leather straps across the top to keep one's feet from falling off when inverted and the control column had a "spade" grip on top. It looked just like what it was called, the handle of a shovel, and was peculiar to every British aircraft I ever flew. The brakes were pneumatic and controlled by a lever in the centre of the "spade." As one squeezed the lever it applied air pressure to the right or left brake as the rudder pedal was pushed or to both when the pedals were neutralized. This feature was standard on most of the operational aircraft in the RAF.

Miles Master III

The instruments were in the usual positions on the panel; however, the U.S. "Inches of mercury" used to measure the manifold pressure had become "pounds of boost," the "needle and ball" was the "slip skid," and the landing gear was the "undercart." The compass was about five inches in diameter and mounted between the knees. It had two parallel lubber lines on the glass face, one end marked in red. The movable verge ring was imprinted with the compass degrees. The parallel lines were set to the desired heading, and the aircraft was turned until an arrow on the red mark was in alignment. Very clever, once it was set; the pilot didn't have to read numbers and could check his course with just a glance.

Then there was the Sutton harness. It was attached at five points, unlike the usual U.S. lap belt, which had no shoulder restraints to prevent the pilot from lurching forward into the instrument panel with predictable results. The Sutton harness had straps over the shoulders as well as over the lap. They were so efficient that there were instances when a pilot, who had been catapulted out of the cockpit in a crash, was found still strapped in his seat, in one piece, alive!

We sat on a dinghy atop a parachute and wore a Mae West, the life vest that when inflated, gave one the shape of that famous, large-bosomed movie actress. It was attached to the life-raft package by a lanyard. In the event of a parachute descent over water, the pilot hit the chute's quick release ring when about ten feet above the surface and fell free, trusting he wouldn't become entangled in the shrouds. Once in the water, he pulled the dinghy inflation lever and crawled in. Almost every Sunday afternoon "dinghy drill" took place in the town's indoor swimming pool. The first time it was rather fun, but it got old in a hurry since we had to wear full flying gear, which had to be dried over night.

With F/Sgt Engineer in the rear, the chocks were pulled and we taxied out, "S" turning in order to see over the long nose of the inline Kestrel engine. We flew about for a while getting the feel of the thing and made several "circuits and bumps." It must have gone pretty well, because after an hour he crawled out, and I was sent solo. That afternoon, with no ceremony, I was given a log book, and nothing more was said about my previous flight training, or lack of it. I was in! It was December the 23rd and a great Christmas present!

A lot of the staff had left for the holidays, but there were many more staying behind. Most of us "friendly aliens" weren't offered leave, but that didn't seem to matter as we didn't have anywhere to go anyway. There was much talk about a party on Boxing Day (the day after Christmas), and much activity in the main mess;

rearranging of furniture and placing of greenery everywhere. But because of government regulations against tree cutting, only a small potted evergreen tree was decorated. It occurred to me that many of those who were entitled to leave stayed because of the impending party. It wasn't often in those dark, grim days of rationing and austerity that there was a chance of attending such a function.

Christmas Day would have been sad for me had it not been for Vern Lewis. It was cold and damp and the day started with "church parade." All of the station personnel, officers and airmen alike, except for a small duty force on watch, were expected to attend. Known as "square bashing," this performance took place every Sunday and Christmas Day on a two-acre paved square in front of station headquarters. Everyone was supposed to stand at attention in the freezing cold while the station Padre, or "sky pilot," read several lengthy passages from the Bible. This was a Church of England religious ceremony, and when everyone was assembled, the station Warrant Officer shouted in a voice that all could hear, "Fall out all non-Christians and Jews."

I was standing next to Vern who whispered, "They don't know what we are. Follow me." With that, he wheeled about with me in tow, and we marched, two abreast, back and forth behind the others along with the authentic non-Christians and Jews. We kept a lot warmer than those standing still in that freezing air, and from then on, we never remained in a church parade, and were never challenged about it.

The British forces had a long-standing tradition that required all officers to attend and serve the troops or airmen at their evening Christmas Eve dinner. A lot of the girls were very attractive, and I must admit, a bit of fraternization took place. We walked them back to their quarters in the dark, with the WAAF officers, or "queen bees," squawking like a flock of hens trying to get their chicks safely back to roost. The darkness caused by the absolute blackout didn't help a bit.

As one might guess, Vern was in great demand. With at least a half dozen girls vying for his attention during dinner, one could be sure he wouldn't walk alone afterward. I don't know what took place, but he was a real mess when he showed up in the hut long after midnight with a stupid grin on his face. It was then I remembered he had told me his wife was coming for the party the next night and he wanted me to help entertain her. I was worried that I might be "stuck" for the entire evening. I could have saved myself a sleepless night had I known then what I found out later.

It really was a party. Those in the service were all in uniform, blue for RAF, dark blue for Navy, and khaki for Army. The locals wore tweeds or party dresses. The place was crowded, noisy and smoke filled, and as I looked around at everyone enjoying themselves, I had the lonesome feeling of being left out. It was not nostalgia; I was never homesick, but I really didn't know anyone other than Vern, and he was nowhere in sight.

There was a tap on my shoulder, and I turned to stare into the most incredible pair of blue eyes I had ever seen. She was very carefully made up, dark haired and had an unbelievable figure. She smiled and said, "You must be Smithy, the Yank Vern has been telling me about. Merry Christmas!" With that she wrapped her arms around my neck and kissed me. I must say, being a country boy from Richmond, I had never experienced anything its equal. It was like being hit in the face with a wet plunger, and she didn't stop at my mouth, but included my eyes, ears, cheeks and then returned to my mouth. It must have continued a full two minutes before I felt her begin to tremble with what I thought was passion. I opened my eyes and darned if she wasn't laughing, and everyone staring! Vern, standing behind her, had put her up to it. He had failed to mention that his wife was a very popular actress on the London stage.

She was a wonderful sport, and I confess, I enjoyed the joke immensely. Her name was Joyce, and we got along famously. She never left my side the whole evening, while Vern "tom-catted" about with some of his WAAF friends. I thought he was deranged to leave her like that, but she explained that they had some sort of "agreement," and I never asked what it was. In any event, her performance in wishing me a merry Christmas made me somewhat of a celebrity, and Vern and I never told the others about the setup. The two of them left long after midnight when the party broke up, and I never saw her again. It was probably just as well.

The orchestra did its job in the mess, but it had considerable competition from the snooker room. Someone was playing the piano and was surrounded by a group singing, "Twas on the good ship Venus, my God you should have seen us, the figurehead was a whore in bed and the mast a rampant..." and more of the raunchiest ditties I had ever heard; "Roll me Over in the Clover," "Little Sunny Jim," "The Scottish Wedding Song," and the worst of all, "Frigging in the Rigging," which contained such verses as, "The Captain had a daughter who fell into the water, you could tell from the squeals of ecstatic eels they had found her..." I was more than mildly surprised to note that there were many WAAF officers in the group, all singing as lustily as the men. The piano player was a WAAF Section Officer.

Flying continued for the next four weeks, but due to the almost always inclement weather, I accumulated only twenty-four hours, ten of which were solo, and one at night.

In daylight, night flying was practiced in a novel way. The runway and taxiways were lined with sodium lamps and the instrument panel lit with fluorescent lights. The pilot wore special dark goggles that blocked out everything except the instruments and the lamps. It was a splendid exercise and a great deal more difficult than the actual night flying we had at home. Night time in England was as black as the inside of a closet. Usually there was no moon, no horizon and not a pinpoint of light, so once one left the hooded runway lights, one was on instruments. Fortunately, we had more time to practice later, but it was something that had to be done correctly each time, "or else..."

Flying the Master Mark I was the first step at Tern Hill; the next was the Master Mark III. The pointed nose of the Kestrel in the Mark I gave way in the Mark III to a huge radial Bristol engine, giving it a brutish look and an awesome sound when the throttle was wide open at full power. More austere and more powerful, yet very much like the AT 6, it was a lot of fun to fly.

Radio transmitter (R/T) procedures were a puzzle. They used a voice-activated microphone set into the face mask. One had to say, "hello, hello" to break open the transmitter and then give a message. The terminology was quite different: Altitude was referred to as "angels," "bandits" were the enemy, "bogy," an unknown aircraft. "Buster" meant as soon as possible and "gate," full throttle at emergency power. Instructions to "pancake" meant to land as soon as possible, without a "prang," or crash. It took me a while to master all this jargon, but when I realized how important it could be, I became a quick learner.

One night we were jerked out of a sound sleep as the Tannoy blasted out that all station personnel were to assemble in one of the hangars by 2:30 am.

Having no idea what it was all about, I quickly dressed and joined the mob headed down hill in the pitch-black darkness. We entered through the blackout curtains of one of the small hangar doors into an enormous hangar completely empty of aircraft but filled with 800 to 1,000 officers and enlisted personnel, all at attention and in complete silence. The hangar was lit by one unshaded light bulb suspended from the fifty-foot ceiling over a single desk, behind which was seated the Station Commanding Officer. The bulb was swinging slightly, casting moving shadows, giving the scene an eerie quality.

As we waited, there was an echo of stamping feet and the loud voice of the station Warrant Officer counting cadence. An airman was marching in front of him with his cap tucked under his right epaulet, indicating, I supposed, that he was in big trouble. We couldn't hear what was said, but in a very few minutes, the prisoner was turned about and marched out with the bellowing voice of the Warrant Officer again shouting cadence. We learned next day that he was given 30-days "jankers" in the "slammer" or "glasshouse" for "pinching" (stealing) a light bulb to replace his, which had expired! Much ado about nothing!

13. The Worst Station in Britain?

After four weeks of "luxury" at Tern Hill, I was posted to Calveley. What a disaster! This place, without question, was the worst station in the British Isles. Everyone who had the same posting agreed. The lack of walkways or paved areas around the barracks, combined with the incessant rains and ever-present dampness, assured that it was forever ankle deep in mud. This was January and as cold as England could get. There was no heat in my small room, no place to stow one's gear and no batman to help. The food was as bad as it could be.

I had a terrible cold and reported to the MO's hut for treatment, only to be told by his WAAF assistants that the doctor was unavailable, that he was in the next room passed out, but they would be glad to treat me. I didn't take long to realize the "assistants" were nymphomaniacs. They gave me a copy of *Eskimo Nell*, suggesting I read it, and bring it back that evening for a "really good time!" Being as cold as I was, the thought of being in bed with a couple of warm female bodies was mighty tempting. But a court martial resulting from being caught in bed playing "slap and tickle" with two WAAFs wasn't exactly what I needed.

I read the story, as nasty as any could be, put it in a paper bag and gave it to a strapping Corporal with instructions to return it that evening to the girls in the MO's office. The next morning when I passed the girls, their faces were wreathed in smiles, and later I got a very proper salute from the Corporal.

Like Harrogate, Calveley was used as a holding place for those with a problem. This seemed to apply to the permanent station administration but not to the flying personnel. We were there awaiting posting to an OTU while making room for another class at Tern Hill. We continued flying the Mark III, mostly at night.

At Calveley, the runway was lit at night with gooseneck kerosene flare pots that were tended by "erks" (ground crew) on bicycles. These pots were quite useful, but trouble began when an air raid alert was sounded. They had to race down the runway on bicycles from each end, snuffing out the flares, leaving some poor beggar aloft circling in the dark until the "all clear" was sounded, and the pots re-lighted. When these "snuffers" were a mix of airmen and WAAFs, it would take twice as long for them to return. Usually out of breath, they would claim they couldn't find their way back in the dark.

My lack of military training was discovered when I was asked to parade the ground crew down to Flights. A Flight Sergeant had about fifty airmen standing at attention waiting for me. I stepped to the head of the parade, in my best commanding voice shouted "Forward March!" and marched off, expecting to hear the sound of marching feet. Silence! I looked back. No one had moved. The Sergeant, a nice chap, slightly red in the face, said, "Mr. Smith, that is not exactly how we do it…" and with that he turned to the parade and shouted, "By the left… quick march!" and off we went.

Except for a few "check rides," most of my instruction was given by a New Zealander named Sergeant Taylor. He hadn't been home for two years and the constant strain of his flight duties had given him a rather severe case of the "twitch." He hated flying, but we got along well.

He and I were sitting with some others in front of Flights waiting for the next available aircraft when two Spitfires with American markings approached from out of nowhere flying in close formation. One broke off and did a perfect loop right over the centre of the aerodrome, then both landed and taxied up to where we were sitting. I was impressed; these were the first "real live" Spitfires I had seen on the ground.

After the engines were shut down, the little doors on the sides opened revealing two US Army Air Force Second Lieutenants. One leaned out and spoke to one of the "erks" who turned and shouted, "Pilot Officer Smith, they want you." Excited, I strolled over trying to look nonchalant, and as I drew closer, I recognized Andy Anderson and my old friend, Doug Munson. They had gotten to England a few weeks before me and had been persuaded to transfer over to the American air forces. They were stationed about fifty miles to the north. Hearing that I had been sent over as the last American to join the RAF, they checked with the American Eagle Club in London and Mrs Dexter, bless her heart, overheard them asking for me and gave them my location.

They were able to stay for only a very few minutes, and most of their time was spent trying to convince me to transfer over to the USAAF. The difference in flight pay was their main point. Theirs was about $420 per month and mine, as an equal in rank, was (in Pounds) about $96. They took off in formation, made a low pass over the runway, and disappeared off to the north. I never saw either again, and to today have no idea if they survived. I don't believe I ever regretted not accepting their advice, but it would have been nice to fly again with people I knew, and had trained with.

A signal came through and I was plucked from the group and, alone, posted to No. 41 Operational Training Unit, Hawarden, North Wales, near the town of Chester. As I was leaving Calveley, the chief flying instructor, Squadron Leader Doug Halfrin, stamped his assessment of my flying ability in my log book. It read, "Pilot above average". Great!

14. No. 41 OTU Hawarden

Hawarden was an enormous aerodrome with a maintenance unit for Vicker's Wellington bombers (known as Wimpys) on one side and our No.41 OTU on the other. Though we were still in Training Command there was a great deal less 'bull' in the OTUs than in the AFUs, probably because all of the staff were ex-operational types and had already been 'put through the mill'.

Our huts had single rooms with the same old iron stove, dresser and washstand and were located along with the mess about a mile from the Flights area down on the airfield. Set on the top of a foothill of the Welsh mountains, just below the small hamlet of Hawarden, it must have been one of the coldest spots in all of the UK, and we were still rationed to those three lumps of coal. The mess had the usual snooker room, a dining room and an anteroom with a bar. Battledress was accepted in the mess at breakfast, lunch and tea, but here too, no flying gear was allowed and one usually dressed in best blues for dinner.

I was at Hawarden for sixty days, which gave me my first opportunity to get to know some of my fellow pilots, who were the usual mix of Irish, Canadian, Australian, Norwegian, Scots, French, South African and many other nationalities. Some loved flying and some hated it. It must have been dreadful to know that one day you were going to have to face an enemy who would do his best to kill you, and at the same time, live in constant fear of being in the air. Those who stuck with it were the real heroes.

Training was begun in the 'Harvard', as it was known in the RAF. It was really an early version of the AT6 we had flown in the States, except it had a fabric-covered fuselage. After two circuits and bumps with Flying Officer Slade, I was sent off solo. This was typical of the British style of training. Not a moment of time or ounce of fuel was wasted.

One of the first Mustangs – Hawarden 1942.

After five or six hours of navigational training and formation flying, we were introduced to the P-51. These were originally built for the US Air Force. They had been designed and manufactured in a little over ninety days by North American Aviation Company as a "marriage" of the Luftwaffe's Me109 and the US P-40. They were powered by an Allison inline engine with a Curtis electric airscrew. The canopy had to remain locked, not only in the air, but for takeoff and landing as well. This 'Mark I' proved to be so unsatisfactory that the US gave most to the RAF. North American proceeded to redevelop the original until it became one of the most efficient long-range fighters of the war.

This was due mostly to the replacement of the Allison by the Rolls Royce Merlin engine.

The P-51 'Mustang' was a single-seater and the first aircraft we were to fly without any previous dual instruction. The 'checkout' was done in the usual RAF manner. We arrived at Flights early one snowy morning and there it sat. It was big! A Flight Sergeant showed us all the 'tits, taps and levers', gave us the takeoff, cruise and approach speeds as well as the maximum temperatures and starting and stopping procedures. He asked, "Any Questions?" There was no response. He asked, "Who is first?" Not a hand was raised. Then he said, "All right, Mr Smith you are the most familiar with the Harvard (also manufactured by North American.) Have a go at it."

This wasn't the way I thought it ought to be, but I, not too enthusiastically, climbed in. The first thing I noted was the "stick" instead of the spade grip control column. Switching back and forth between the two types wasn't a problem, but one had to think before applying brakes. The Mustang had toe brakes on the rudder pedals instead of the lever in the spade.

An erk assisted with the straps and buckles and when I was settled, he pulled the canopy forward and pushed a small lever which locked it, a clear reminder that the only way it could be opened in flight was to jettison it … and the tail would probably go along with it!

Nevertheless, I started the engine, the chocks were removed, and I began a long, snaking taxi around the perimeter track leading to a runway that paralleled the River Dee. I came to a stop in the holding area and, while waiting for a green light from the control tower, went through the standard cockpit drill for takeoff (TMPFFG: throttle nut tightened, mixture full rich, pitch fully fine, fuel on, flaps lowered 15 degrees, gills for the radiator open.)

Finally, I was given a green light and as I moved into position, I noticed a flock of terns or sea gulls wandering about in the middle of the runway. They scattered as I slowly opened up to full throttle, and began what soon became a rush. The thing leaped forward until we were tearing down the runway at an incredible speed. It wanted to fly a lot sooner than I thought it should, and as I eased back on the control column it immediately came unstuck.

Once airborne, it behaved like any other aircraft, maybe a little heavier on the controls, but with no unexpected surprises and very fast. Wheels and flaps up, it gained speed rapidly and I was very quickly out of the circuit and over the practice area. After reaching 2000 feet and executing a few quick turns and a stall or two, I felt quite at home.

Just to my left I noticed a Hurricane forming up on my wing tip. The pilot was obviously curious because there weren't many P-51s around at the time. I had been loafing at about half throttle when he joined me. I gradually increased power until he began to fall astern, then applied full power. He must have been startled at the speed as I slipped away, climbing all the while.

After an hour's flight and a few circuits and bumps, I returned to Flights, rather pleased with myself, and faced a barrage of questions about its performance from the other students. To my surprise, the Flight Commander handed me an evaluation sheet containing all sorts of technical questions which took an hour to complete. This, I assumed, was to help with further development of the type, since each of us was required to write it up after every flight.

We flew these about thirty hours flat out at or below tree level, practicing low-level map reading for reconnaissance along the French coast. It was rather exciting watching the landscape go by at 250 to 300 miles per hour at zero feet. In our sizable practice area, there was no limitation on height or speed other than that dictated by the occasional copse of trees.

A visiting Group Captain, having heard about the quickness of the Mustang, arrived at Flights and insisted he be allowed to have a "go" at it. He was an exuberant fellow with several "gongs" on his tunic and loved to fly. He was given the usual briefing and away he went. On his return he taxied up to the dispersal area and leaped out of the cockpit. He was so impressed he was actually dancing with excitement.

The Flight Commander calmed him down and handed him the evaluation sheet with the request that he fill it in. He looked at it for a minute, reached across the desk for a large black crayon, and scrawled across the sheet (and I paraphrase) – *She goes like manure off a shovel with little more noise than a duck's flatulence* – and signed it. I have often wondered about the looks on the faces at Air Ministry when his evaluation showed up in the "Most Secret" pouch.

There were several minor prangs and one major one. Flight Lieutenant Varley flew through a flock of those bloody seagulls on takeoff. They crashed through the leading edge of his wing and also plugged up the air intake of his engine. Trying to go around, he lost altitude due to the damage to his wing, but probably could have made it had his engine not quit entirely. He pranged into a copse of trees at the end of the runway and ploughed through two so close together that they sheared off not only his main wings but the horizontal tailplane as well. The fuselage continued for another hundred yards fairly undamaged until it slid into a hill and caught fire. We never knew how, but he managed to get out. He was found lying on the ground, badly burned, dead, with nearly every bone in his body broken.

Casualties began to mount; causes were equally divided between pilot error and equipment failure.

Captain Tufft Johnson of the Royal Norwegian Air Force, whose room was next to mine, was a very quiet-spoken chap and of some importance, judging by the way he was treated by the senior officers. He was usually very casual and calm but one morning following a crash landing (prang) he had the day before, I passed by him sitting on his front stoop in a robe and pyjamas with a dazed look on his face, smoking a cigarette.

I stopped to speak and when I noticed he was trembling, I sat down beside him to see if I could help. He told me he had had a nightmare. He dreamt he was invited to a dinner in his honour and when he arrived he found a dozen or more old friends whom he recognized as having been killed. They were all seated around a banquet table with one empty chair and a place card which he didn't bother to read. The chap at the head of the table asked why he was late. They had been *waiting for him to join them!*

Fast forward to 1989. Alice and I were in Oslo and I found the name General Tufft Johnson in a phone book. Out of curiosity, I called to see if it could be my old friend. The lady who answered the phone spoke English quite well and identified herself as Tufft's wife. I told her I had been with him at Hawarden in 1942 but hadn't seen or heard from him since. She remembered his being at No. 41 OTU. She was English and they had been married in London just after he completed the course at Hawarden. Then she did the oddest thing. She asked if I would like to speak to him. When I said that I would, she told me he had died of lung cancer six months before! I was so taken aback that I could only thank her and hang up.

Late one afternoon, a signal came through from Air Ministry asking for volunteers for posting to the Middle East. Realizing most of the fighter Squadrons in England had at that time a full complement, and that OTU training would continue until there were vacancies, I, along with some others, mostly Canadians, volunteered, hoping to fly Spitfires that much sooner.

We were all Pilot Officers (P/Os): Dave McBride, Bruce Evans, Paul Doig, Gavin Adams, Walter Lock, Jock McCloud, Jim Ward, Tony Golab, and Jake Woolgar are some that I can remember.

They were being used in the North African desert, so for the next four days we flew Hawker Hurricanes. All had fabric-covered fuselages and metal wings containing eight .303 machine guns in the leading edges. They were very stable, clumsy looking, slow, but tough machines that were fun to fly. They could out-turn just about anything in the air. This was important, as the "Jerries" found out. Their 109s couldn't turn tight enough to get inside for a deflection shot, and the "Hurryboxes" could carry on until they had a chance for a shot or the 109 broke away. These "ugly ducklings" were largely responsible for keeping the invaders at bay during the battle of Britain. Manufacture of the Spitfire had just begun, and there were only a few Squadrons fortunate enough to be equipped with those marvellous machines at the time. My guess is the ratio of Hurricane Squadrons to Spitfire Squadrons was close to two to one in favour of the Hurricane.

My first flight almost became a disaster. As usual, the checkout was brief: "this is how you start it, this is how you stop it, the undercart lever is on the right. Be *sure* to select "wheels up" as soon as you are airborne or you might get a hydraulic lock, and have trouble lowering them for landing." Off I went, selected "wheels up" as soon as we left the ground, flew around the circuit, and then attempted to go through the landing drill (UMPFFG: undercarriage down, mixture rich, pitch fine, fuel supply, flaps down, gills on radiator open). When I tried to move the undercarriage lever it wouldn't budge. Hydraulic lock! By then I was on final approach with no wheels. The Aerodrome

Control Pilot (ACP) shot up a red flare from his "Very pistol," and I pulled up, flew past the tower and banked so they would see the wheels were stuck.

As I passed, I looked behind and saw the "meat wagon" on the way out to the runway. What a mess! My only recourse was a wheels-up landing in the grass alongside the active runway. I went through what I thought was the proper procedure; flaps down, canopy locked open, seat lowered, harness as tight as possible, hand on the ignition switch, and lined myself up with the grass strip.

By now I was pretty annoyed. At about twenty feet I gave the lever one more good whack, hitting it on the top. It slid obediently forward and I got the "wheels down" green light just before touchdown. The instructor had neglected to tell me the gear lever was spring loaded in a ratchet and had to be depressed to operate for "Down." The silly clot had never flown this Mark of Hurricane. I often wondered how many aircraft, as well as lives, had been lost due to such poor indoctrination.

15. An Aerial Display

One grey afternoon, the Tannoy announced there was to be an aerial demonstration of the Spitfire and all students and instructors were to report to the front of the control tower at 3:00 pm. It was raining, and the ceiling couldn't have been more than 2000 feet, but we all walked down to the aerodrome as ordered and milled about for the better part of an hour waiting for the display which was to be flown by a chap named Alex Henshaw – Supermarine's chief test pilot.

Word had gotten out that it was very difficult to handle in the air as well as on the ground, and this demonstration was to dispel any such rumours. Standing there in the pouring rain, it was hard to believe anyone could even find the place, much less put up an acceptable show. We had given up, and started back to the mess when there was a shout.

There, only dimly seen through the rain and mist, was a Spitfire coming flat out, headed in our direction, no higher than the hangar roofs. There must have been a signal given, for just as Henshaw hove into sight, a Wellington bomber took off from the other side of the 'drome. The "Spit" dove to the attack and began the wildest "rat race" I had ever witnessed. The pilot of the Wellington was one of the best. I think it was "Mutt" Summers, a test pilot and friend of Henshaw, who had spent years testing and developing the bomber. They chased each other around and between the hangars from one end of the aerodrome to the other, sometimes no more than fifty yards apart and so low that they disappeared below the tops of the buildings. This continued for five or ten minutes until the Wellington broke off, and Henshaw began his demonstration.

I'm sure he won't mind if I paraphrase from his popular book, *Sigh for a Merlin:*

> "If I received a request from an OTU, I would of course be pleased to go. The first visit was to Hawarden, which had become one of the most important OTUs in the country for final training. Here, as well as trainees, were some of the best pilots in the Air Force. I was fully aware that whilst I might have got away creditably with some wild gyrations in front of an ill-informed group, this time my audience would be critical. In fact, some might welcome the opportunity to pick holes in a young amateur.
>
> "The drill was to take off and not climb but pause with the wheels coming up, then at 150 ias (indicated air speed) pull up slowly into a half loop, roll out and repeat this until I was at altitude. Then, placing myself over the aerodrome, do a half roll and go into an absolutely vertical dive with full engine and maximum revs to pull up a few feet from the ground and go into an upward vertical roll to the right and a half roll to the left, pulling out in another half roll. The throttle would be snapped back and plummeting down one could get in two complete aileron turns to pull out, open the throttle and repeat in the opposite direction."

I saw these manoeuvres; his vertical dive took him below the hangars and when he pulled up, he disappeared in the overcast. There was an audible gasp from the crowd, thinking he was now in real trouble, but seconds later down he came, spot on, and continued the show. He wrote further:

> "I could usually get one and a half to two flick-rolls on the horizontal and while I have never seen anyone flick-roll a Spit-

*fire I must say I have always found it a bit frightening to abuse
a machine and have it flash out of your control, if only for a
few seconds, like a spirited blood-horse. I would go inverted
and push the machine into an almost vertical climb and then
as it lost momentum from the negative G position pull the controls gently over to form a half loop hoping the engine would
burst into life as I opened the throttle. This it usually did with
a spectacular sheet of flame pluming from the exhaust stubs
caused by the excess fuel which had accumulated during the
inverted maneuvers. Then with the engine at full power I
would roll to the right, then to the left just in front of the audience below hangar height finishing in the inverted position,
from which I would "raise" the undercarriage, (it had a pneumatic system so the wheels would dramatically "pop" up), go
into a fast inverted turn, lower the flaps as I rolled upright and
touched down for the landing."*

After his display, Henshaw stayed for a few minutes to speak
to the Station Commander, then took off again and disappeared
in the rain as he headed back to Castle Bromwich. I have seen
many aerobatic performances in all types of modern aircraft, but
never one to match his of more than sixty years ago.

*Alice and I have kept in touch with Alex and his wife, Barbara, for
many years. A more delightful couple could never be found. Alex was
recently honored as the recipient of an MBE presented in Court by
Prince Phillip, but sadly, Barbara succumbed after a long battle with
a rare blood disease.*

Alex Heshaw in conversation with Sir Winston Churchill.

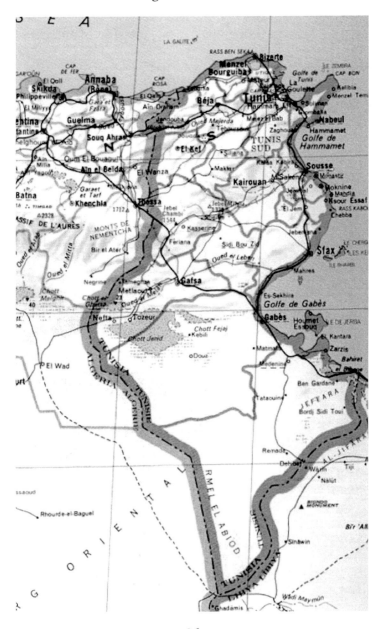

16. To Africa

It was early April 1943 when the signal came through posting us to Africa, and two days later we were off to Blackpool for equipment, immunization shots and tropical gear. We were billeted in an old apartment building right across the street from the pier and the famous Blackpool Tower, which was known all over Britain as a favourite spot for honeymooners and summer vacationers. Now it was deserted and looked rather drab, and in need of a new paint job.

On the stairway of one of the apartments, we joined a continuous line of airmen standing to one side on each step, left arms bared for the shots being given by two medical orderlies located on the top floor. On the other side of the stairway were those descending from the treatment upstairs. Noticing the rate at which they were coming down, some wag in our line suggested the orderlies must be operating with four hands each. I reached the top behind a large Flight Sergeant, and was more than interested in the speed and the devil-may-care attitude of the two doing the sticking.

There was a pile of syringes with needles the size of those used for horses, each being refuelled without benefit of re-sterilization that we could see. These were handed to the main operator who said, "This ain't gonna hurt a bit, Chum," as he lunged at the victim. The Flight Sergeant turned his head as he took his "hit" and was starting to move away when I tapped him on the shoulder and called his attention to the needle still stuck in his arm. The orderly took a pair of pincers and drew it out and the Flight Sergeant hit the floor in a dead faint.

I decided this was no place for me and turned to go, but the little bugger was too quick and I got mine as I was stepping over the inert body of the Flight Sergeant being dragged aside. It was a long trip down those stairs and I confess I was hugging the wall all the way until I finally got outside in the fresh air. This episode, with the exception of bouts with sand-fly fever and hay fever, was the last time in four and one-half years that I had any contact with an MO or had any sort of medical exam. Lucky, I guess.

Tropical equipment was issued that afternoon in a large arena. All pilots were issued calf-length, suede, lightweight sand boots, khaki knee-length socks, shorts and shirts, topees and canvas flying helmets with a flap in the back to prevent neck sunburn. Each was also given what was called a "camp kit," consisting of a collapsible canvas chair, washstand, *bathtub,* and sleeping cot, all rolled up in a woollen blanket. This was wrapped in a heavy canvas cover held together by two leather straps with a carrying handle. The whole thing must have weighed at least sixty pounds, but it was very useful when set up on site in a tent. However, getting it there along with a kit bag containing all of one's worldly possessions, was a problem. More about this later when we arrive in Africa.

Our departure in the rain the next day on HMS *Duchess of Kent* was almost delayed by the struggle to get all the equipment on board. The weight, combined with the soreness of our left arms, made it rather difficult to carry.

The ship, known as "the Drunken Duchess" because of its rolling motion in any kind of sea, was jammed. Every inch of space was taken in the cabins and even the "hold" was filled with men. There was much discontent when it was learned that an ENSA troop of entertainers, some of them women, were given the best of the first class accommodations, two to a cabin. They tried to give several evening shows but, being half drunk, they were so awful that no one watched. They finally gave up and retired to their cabins for their never-ending parties of booze and "Slap and tickle." It's a shame that time, space, equipment and food had to be wasted on this lot. They were a crummy bunch, not at all like some of the other dedicated entertainers.

There were only a dozen or so of us pilots on board and we were called upon to stand what was known as "aircraft recognition watch" night and day. I never found out what we were supposed to do if we saw an aircraft that wasn't ours. The convoy escorts were so far away they could never reach us in time to prevent an air strike, so about all we could do would be to give a warning and don our life jackets.

Another fascinating duty was "torpedo watch" at night. About two hundred men were sleeping down in the bowels of the ship. Regulations required they not be on deck after nightfall, and one officer was to "sleep" at the foot of the ladder leading to the upper deck. The idea was that this "brave officer" would lead the men to safety should one of the things hit. We were rotated, and my turn in the hold didn't come until we were just entering the Mediterranean off the coast of Gibraltar, and the escort corvettes had notified the convoy of submarine activity in the area.

It was hot as blazes when I took my bed roll down into the hold. What a stench! All of those unwashed bodies combined with the smell of vomit, temporary latrines and clouds of cigarette smoke were enough to make one *wish* for a torpedo strike. Poor lads. It certainly gave me some insight into the hardships the non-commissioned troops had to undergo. I don't think any of us got much sleep that night.

17. Algiers & a Sneezing Fit

The sight of the city of Algiers in the early morning sunrise was breathtaking. From the harbour it looked sparkling, white and pristine with its domed mosques and minaret towers glistening in the sun, just as I had pictured it when reading *Arabian Nights*. But the harbour itself was choked with half sunken landing craft, bits and pieces of trucks, oil, garbage, and other debris left over from the landings a few months before; a real mess.

Hundreds of locals, some in flowing white burnooses and Arab headgear and others in mere rags, were waiting on the quay hoping to sell their wares or be of some service as guides or luggage bearers. We had been told to beware, that should one allow them to so much as touch a piece of kit, it would be gone in an instant. The British throughout the Middle East referred to these people as "effing wogs" (wily oriental gentlemen), and we were advised that it was best to stay clear of them and do our own toting.

As we moved out of the ship and down the gangplank, it felt as though someone had opened a furnace door. It was a dry heat, at least 120 degrees in the sun and never below 100 degrees in the shade during the day. I was in the last section to disembark, and when I reached the quay there were sixty airmen there, drawn up in formation, each carrying his desert kit and all his personal belongings. A Wing Commander Administration, with a clipboard in hand, scurried up, and told me that since I was the only general duties (flying) officer available and outranked those who were non-flying, I was in charge of getting these sixty airmen to Maison Currie.

Maison Currie was said to be about ten miles down the road. In this heat, carrying all this luggage, with no food and very little water, I doubted we would ever make it, but we set off in loose formation with a Flight Sergeant in charge of the men. After the first few miles, some began dropping out, and were told to rest and follow along when they felt better. There wasn't much chance of getting lost. There was only the one long straight road in the dust, leading off into the distance. There was not a tree or house in sight anywhere. We pressed on until late afternoon, stopping every half hour for a five-minute rest.

Maison Currie hadn't come into view by dark, so we halted in front of what appeared to be an abandoned brick yard where there were a few sheds covering some drying racks. These racks were in layers about two feet apart so that one could stretch out in relative comfort, out of the dust and dirt and what was left of the heat of the day.

Our water was held in canvas bags and kept tepid (not cool) by evaporation. (By the time I left Africa, cool water had become an obsession and I promised myself I would never pass a water cooler again without stopping for a drink; and I don't.) There was enough for everyone to ease his thirst. That and a cigarette were all the enjoyment to be had as the day dwindled into twilight. The men were sitting around grousing about the lack of rations, although most agreed it was too hot to eat.

Off about a hundred yards, I noticed a queue of a dozen or so airmen waiting in front of a small tent, which I took to be a latrine. I complemented the Flight Sergeant on having one set up so quickly and asked him where he had secured the tent. He laughed and said, "Mr. Smith, that's not a latrine. It's an Arab woman charging arf a quid for a 'go' at it. She and her husband have been following us ever since we left Algiers and he set up the tent within a half hour of our arrival." Now what was I supposed to do, other than suggest he see that the men attend a "short-arm inspection" as soon as possible.

At sunup, with much horn blowing, two lorries arrived in a cloud of dust with rations, and the information that we were supposed to be at Blida Aerodrome, in the opposite direction. This meant we had to retrace our steps to the suburbs of Algiers. This time, however, we had the use of the lorries for both the equipment and the men.

During the past few years I had suffered with what was diagnosed as hay fever. During the night I had started sneezing due to the dust and this continued the next morning with such frequency that I was unable to eat. It had reached the point where I was exploding every thirty seconds and finding it difficult to keep my eyes open. The ride back to Blida was torture. The flies, the dust, the glaring sun, and the heat all added to my misery. I scarcely recall our arrival.

Blida had been a flying school for the French before the war and was built for life in that climate. Bare tiled floors, and thick whitewashed cement walls did much to keep the heat at a minimum and the whole place had been swept clean. The only room with any furniture was up on the second floor; it had stools and tables and a long marble bar.

One of the batmen set up my camp kit and helped me to bed. By now I was weak from the constant sneezing. I was exhausted and wanted to do nothing but sleep. It was impossible, and by the next morning, I was in bad shape. Some kind soul drove me to the hospital about two miles down the road and deposited me in the doorway. By then I was unable to stand, and one of the orderlies wheeled me on a gurney into a cool, quiet room. I was impressed by the immediate appearance of an RAF MO, a Flight Lieutenant who, after a few questions, went right to work.

I was obviously dehydrated, but he took care of that with injections of saline. He said he would like to try a new treatment he had recently heard about. What choice did I have? With my permission, he injected what he described as "pyrobenzamine" directly into a muscle in my arm. (I still have its name written in a small notebook that I carried throughout the war.) Within the hour the sneezing had stopped. What a relief! The MO had told me to stay in bed until the next morning, but I was feeling so well in an hour or so that I decided to walk back to the station.

I stepped out of the front door, and the temperature was at least 130 degrees in the sun. I made it about a quarter of the way back, where one of the lads returning from Algiers in a van found me in a ditch, out cold, and kindly delivered me to my batman. Remarkably, from that day forward, I never had another attack.

Paul Doig and Smithy, Surcouf, Algeria (notice the tin helmet).

18. Algerian Escapades

As previously mentioned, Blida had been a flying school for the French. These fellows, "Free French," had agreed to assist the French Foreign Legion for three years in return for flight training. After war was declared and France had fallen, those who had been trained tried to form what was to be known as the "Lafayette Escadrille" to operate under the Free French banner. More about that later.

My mates from Hawarden were already there when I arrived, and we were all mustered into what was called "Ferry Command." There were about eight or ten clapped out Hurricanes on the aerodrome, a few old French relics and a Squadron of Fleet Air Arm Coastal Command Lockheed Hudsons used for anti-submarine patrol.

The runway was made up of interlocking, perforated steel plating, known as "PSP," laid over the dust and sand and was lit at night with flare pots. The Hudsons provided a great deal of excitement when they returned from their daylight patrols, always after sundown. Their fuel tanks were located just above the landing gear struts and when a poor soul attempting a three-point landing dropped in too hard, the tanks would be punctured by a strut or struts. When the leaked fuel was ignited by the flares, a nasty but spectacular fire would ensue. Most of the time the crews, being aware of this potential, were unbuckled and ready to go. They usually escaped unharmed, but the flames would light up the dark desert for miles around. Wheel landings became the order of the day (or rather the night).

Our Squadron Commander was Flight Lieutenant Alan Hay, DFC, a survivor (one of very few) of a Squadron of what were known as "Hurricats." He was three quarters of the way "round the bend," obviously nervous and strung out, but as nice a chap as one could hope to meet.

The "Hurricat" was a Hurricane mounted on a catapult on the deck of a freighter in front of a convoy. The pilot remained in the cockpit during daylight, warming up the engine every half hour as the convoy neared the coast. Should an enemy aircraft be sighted, he was fired off to the attack. Alas, whether or not he was successful in repelling the bandit, there was no way for him to be retrieved. His only alternatives were to reach land before his fuel was exhausted or attempt to ditch alongside a ship and pray for rescue from the icy waters that could kill a man in a matter of minutes. Hay had survived this twice, and when he was told he was entitled to a posting for a rest or perhaps a desk job, he chose North Africa.

Hay not only led us as our Ferry Flight Squadron Leader, but also as our tour guide to every den of iniquity in Algiers, including a place called "The Sphinx" – located deep in the area known as the Casbah, a crowded marketplace in the centre of the city that had the look of something straight out of *Arabian Nights*. We learned later that it was known to every sailor and adventurer the world-over who had ever entered the port, as having the most obscene "exhibishione" (as the locals pronounced it) in the entire world. Later, as a bug-eyed observer, I had to agree.

The Casbah, due to the unpredictable and vicious nature of some of its inhabitants, had been placed "off limits" to all troops, day or night. These creatures were known for their cruelty, lack of regard for life, and insensitivity to the pain they might inflict on others. Even today, there are news reports of atrocities being committed in that same small area of the city. We had read a military police report about two airmen who, when seen on the street trying to coax a woman to lift her veil, were attacked by a crowd of locals. The next morning they were found on the outskirts barely alive, bound hand and foot, with their 'privates' sewn up in their mouths. That should have been a strong enough warning, but it didn't seem to bother Hay a bit and we followed blithely along.

We hadn't any transport, but a freight train ran from Constantine to Algiers at sunset every day, and passed just behind the aerodrome at a speed no quicker than a fast trot. It was made up entirely of cattle cars which one could hardly see because of the hundreds of people jammed inside and hanging onto the outside like "flies on a piece of camel dung." There was a crowd covering the roofs and the coal tender and even the cowcatcher. The term "mass transportation" must have originated here! Five of us, Dave McBride, Walter Lock, Jake Woolgar, our fearless leader Hay and I ran alongside until we managed to get a hand hold and were off to Algiers.

If one could overlook the dirt and filth it was a beautiful city, but overlooking the filth was difficult. It was not uncommon to see three or four of the locals in their flowing, full-length robes, squatting in a circle in animated conversation, then rising and striding off in different directions, leaving behind a pile of human waste.

It had gotten dark, and the narrow cobblestone streets were only dimly lit by the glow of oil lamps in the windows of the crammed-together houses. Ragged little six- to eight-year-old urchins were everywhere, begging for chocolates and cigarettes and offering to lead us to their big sister for "jig-a-jig" or to The Sphinx. We would never have found it on our own. Hidden back among a labyrinth of twisting streets, its unlit, unimposing entrance looked just the same as all the others.

This was the first and only whorehouse I have ever knowingly been in. We entered a smoke-filled room through the traditional bead-curtained doorway to find a bar that must have been fifty feet long. Almost every stool was topped by a beautiful "lady of the evening," nursing a drink, cigarette in hand, head tilted back, exhaling smoke through her nostrils or blowing smoke rings, just like those in the cinema. There were at least twenty of them, mostly Caucasian, each smiling a warm welcome, and we, except for a few Allied sailors, were the only ones in attendance.

Half scared, we approached the bar hesitantly, and each of us was immediately surrounded by a chattering bevy of good-looking girls, almost as if they had been expecting us. Speaking in a mixture of German, English, French, and Arabic, they sounded like another Tower of Babel. Nevertheless, the "international proposition" was easily understood. We all respectfully declined. Not in the slightest dismayed, for a fee of twenty akers from each of us, they agreed to put on "La Exibishione."

We filed down a narrow spiral staircase into a room about thirty by forty feet that contained a flat bed of at least twenty by thirty feet. The "ladies" had their clothes off in a matter of seconds and were "naked as jaybirds." Their performance during the next hour is not to be described here. Suffice it to say that we were exhausted just from observing.

At the conclusion, we all filed back up the spiral staircase. The bare bottom of one of the "ladies" was right in front of McBride's face. I couldn't resist. I reached around Mac and gave it a healthy "goose." She screeched, turned and belted him so hard that he fell backward. Like dominos, we all landed in a heap at the foot of the stairs. Mac, unable to understand her Arabic tirade, was at a complete loss. However, after a glass or two of champagne, she accepted his apology and invited him to join her in one of the back rooms. By then our leader had gotten a "snootful" and decided we had better try to find our way back to the aerodrome.

The next morning, Lock rolled over in bed and said something about dreaming that someone was shouting for help. Still confused from our activities the night before, we dressed and headed for the mess. As we passed one of the air raid slit trenches, we heard a weak, croaking cry for help. Sure enough, our fearless leader had fallen into, and spent the night in the eight-foot trench. It was too deep to climb out of and there had been no ladder and no one sober enough to attend to his cries, poor fellow.

Overseas Pay and Allowances: the pound equaled approx. $4.50, the shilling equaled approx. $0.22

We flew the Hurricanes several times a day practicing shadow firing, low-flying along the edge of the sea, and generally keeping our hand in. The old Hurricane IIc was still great fun to fly. They were slow and cumbersome but with their wide, soft undercarts, they could be landed with eyes closed on almost any type of terrain, sand included.

It was seemingly impossible for them to be overloaded. The antitank versions carried two 40 mm Bofors guns and their heavy rounds of ammunition with little change in flight characteristics. However, several were lost because of an increase in stalling speed caused by the additional weight plus the recoil when the guns were fired. This could cause a high-speed stall when pulling up too sharply after a tank attack.

Early one morning I was sent up for an air test on one of the older machines just out of the maintenance unit (MU). Takeoff was normal but when I selected "wheels up," all hell broke loose. Hydraulic oil sprayed everywhere inside the cockpit. I couldn't make out where it was coming from, and the real problem was not being able to see. My goggles were covered, and I didn't dare take them off, because I had no idea how long the fluid would continue escaping. It stopped after a few minutes but it seemed like hours. I removed my goggles and slammed open the canopy to get a clear view. The indicator lights showed the wheels were down but not locked. I got the port one locked by rocking side to side but the light indicating the starboard wheel position remained red. With no fluid, it was impossible to retract the "good" wheel for a safe belly landing. The only choice was to pull up sharply and hope the centrifugal force would lock the other. It worked and the two little green lights, indicating "Up" glowed pleasantly.

Crossing over the Atlas Mountains on the northern edge of the Sahara, one could see for miles when the noonday sun was directly overhead. The landscape was a vast expanse of nothing but barren desert, usually quiet unless the dreaded sirocco winds began to blow. That was a sight to see. It looked as if the whole desert had lifted up and become ten thousand feet thick. The dust was impenetrable and would very quickly stall and ruin any aircraft engine. Daily routine orders said, "Don't even try it."

Sadly, Tony Hawley got caught in a one and was missing for days. His body was finally found with his Hurricane, both stripped bare by a passing tribe of nomads. To prevent this sort of thing we had been issued a "goolie chit" written in Arabic, stating that a reward of fifty pounds sterling would be paid for the return of the pilot, dead or alive. They must have overlooked his.

The Free French pilots were hanging around with nothing to do but be a "pain in the ass." They kept telling us how great they were and what they would do if they had aircraft to fight the Hun for "poor La Belle France." On the other side of the field, there were two old Potezes (French-built twin-engine bombers) that had been lying uncovered in the sun for at least a year or more. They tinkered with the engines on one for a few days, washed and polished the wings and fuselage, and then announced they were going to fly it to France and join up.

The wings and fuselage were made of glued plywood, and with the two old Rhone engines and dilapidated twin propellers, it looked almost prehistoric. The next morning at about sunup we gathered on the edge of the runway to watch. After much wheezing, coughing and belching of exhaust smoke, the engines came alive, and all six pilots crawled aboard. With throttles wide open, the old Potez slowly moved forward and gathered speed.

At about three quarters of the way down, a rough track crossed the runway. It had been made by the never-ending parade of donkeys and camels being herded to the sea by their drivers, and we always made sure we were airborne before we reached these deep ruts. Well, the adventurers must not have seen it. When they hit the track, the Potez bounced about twenty feet in the air and settled back with such force that it flew into a thousand pieces. Sheets of plywood were flying everywhere.

The Frenchmen hit the ground running, scattering in all directions. Not a one stopped to see if anyone was hurt or trapped inside. This seemed to be typical of them. The RAF had an expression for this attitude: "Screw you Jack, pull up the gang-plank, I'm on board." It took an American bulldozer only a few minutes to scrape the mess to one side, and flying resumed for the day.

We were eagerly awaiting the arrival of a new US Army Air Corps Squadron of P-40s. Tony Hawley (the lad who was later killed in the Sirocco) was the Aerodrome Control Pilot (ACP). He was located about 300 yards down the active runway in a little open-sided hut to protect him from the blistering sun. His duty was to fire a warning with a red flare from a Very pistol or employ a red Aldis lamp when he saw an aircraft about to land on top of another in the clouds of dust. Kicked up from the prop blast, the dust was almost impenetrable and took as much as five minutes to settle on a windless day. Consequently, everyone took off and landed in line-abreast formation or waited until the dust settled.

The new arrivals came roaring down the runway at about one hundred feet: a beautiful formation of P-40 Tomahawks in "Vee" sections of three each. They peeled off, went into line-astern, and headed for the approach end of the runway. Foreseeing what was coming, we held our breath. Sure enough, the leader landed almost opposite Tony and raised the predictable thick cloud of dust. The next landed in clear air just short of the dust, going at a pretty good clip as he disappeared into the cloud. The others kept coming. The next time we saw Tony he was out of the hut, Very pistol in hand, firing red flares, not up in the air but *at* the approaching P-40s.

They seemed to get the message and veered off. Tony told us he couldn't see the second plane but when he heard it he hit the ground as the wing swooped overhead, destroying the hut. He was a pretty even-tempered lad but what really set him off was the pilot's explanation: "I thought I would try to land on instruments!" It was only our restraint that kept Tony from shooting the beggar with the Very pistol.

Hay was concerned about my pay status when compared to that of the US Army Air Corps and suggested that I put in for a transfer. Though he found it difficult to understand, I still felt a loyalty to the RAF and I didn't care to undergo all the training that would be necessary to adapt to the US system. He pressed the point until I finally agreed to apply for transfer to the US Naval Air Corps. I wrote out the request and he signed it, and sent it off to Mediterranean Allied Air Force (MAAF) Headquarters at Constantine. After ten days there had been no response, so he sent off a follow up. Still no reply. He wasn't used to this type of treatment and decided we should follow the paper trail. This meant a trip to Telergma, the nearest aerodrome to Constantine.

Telergma was three hundred miles to the east, a two-hour flight over nothing but desert wasteland. But Hay was determined, so off we went in two clapped-out Hurricanes armed with four .303 machine guns and two 20 mm cannons "just in case." Without incident, we landed line-abreast in the usual cloud of sand and dust and were driven to headquarters by an American Corporal in an American jeep. There were Yanks everywhere. I hadn't seen as many since I left the States.

Headquarters' offices were on the second floor of a two-story building not unlike a present-day motel. We were ushered into a large room filled with filing cabinets and a huge desk manned by a bespectacled master Sergeant. There was a light of recognition in his eyes when we mentioned the transfer request, and he suggested that we see the General. He disappeared into an office across from his and reappeared moments later, leaving the door open and indicating that we were to enter.

The General was standing in front of a window with his back to us as we came to attention and saluted smartly. When he turned I recognized him immediately. The General in command was my boyhood hero, James Doolittle.

We explained our mission. He listened intently and then called the Sergeant and asked, "Sergeant, what do you know about this?" The reply was, "Well, Sir, we had two requests from Mr Smith requesting transfer to the US Naval Air Corps, and as the Navy doesn't have a Flight Surgeon in the area to perform a medical exam, we weren't sure how they should be handled, so they were 'filed in the round file'."

We all just stood there rather dumbfounded. Then General Doolittle asked, "Smith, do you really want to do this thing?"

I said, "General, if it means that I must return to the States to be examined and go through a lot of retraining then, no Sir. We'll drop it." My reply solved the problem and after answering his questions about how I happened to be in the RAF, we saluted, thanked him (I almost asked for his autograph) and flew back to Algiers.

Upon arrival, we were told to pack up. We were to be posted to Setif in two days. We were also told the Queen Bee of the hive of American nurses in Oran had requested an evening's entertainment for her staff and would be arriving that very evening at 6 o'clock with twenty girls. They could stay only a short time because of their curfew and evening meal.

While we had a beautiful bar, the delivery of our supply of booze had been delayed and we were down to only six or eight bottles of gin and no mixers. The British would take soda water, dissolve an anti-malaria quinine tablet in it, and mix it with gin to make the pill's bitter taste more palatable. This became the now fashionable "gin and tonic."

(While on this subject, as long as I was with the RAF, even under the most dire circumstances, I never saw an occasion when one couldn't get a drink or two in the officers' mess. Whisky was a very valuable asset when we were dealing with our thirsty American allies. It was frequently exchanged for sweets, food, personal supplies, and once a Jeep appeared after two cases of Scotch disappeared. An officer's ration was a quart a month, and as there were always some "teetotallers," there was usually a surplus.)

But back to the proposed party. We all went to work sweeping out the place, dusting off the tables and even scrounging some biscuits and cheese for hors d'oeuvres. We were on the second floor so the flies weren't too bad at that time of evening, and after sunset the breeze from the "Med" cooled the place down to a degree that was almost comfortable. The question now was how to become acquainted with and entertain the ladies in such a short period of time. I left that to the others and went back to my room for a bath and clean clothes.

I arrived at the party at 6:30, and as I walked in, I was greeted by several playful, very inebriated nurses. I was puzzled as to how they had gotten such a buzz on so quickly, but I soon found out. On each of the six tables was a carafe of water and several bottles of Gordon's gin. One of our Canadian friends, never at a loss as to how to entertain a lady, had filled the gin bottles with water and the carafes with the colorless gin! Of course, when a nurse was offered a drink her response would be a ladylike, "Just a little gin, please, with lots of water."

Boy, what a mess! For the next-half hour, Queen Bee included, they were fired up like a bunch of coeds on spring break, ready to hug and kiss or whatever with anybody. They were all "so grateful" for such a "lovely party" given by such a "sweet bunch of brave pilots." Little did they realize those "sweet, brave pilots" who spoke with the "charming British accent" wanted nothing more than to "get into their knickers".

It came time to go, and when we ushered them outside to the waiting transport, they and whichever fellows they had their arms around at the time scattered, off into the darkness. The Queen Bee, "pissed as a newt," reminded me of a farmer's wife trying to shoo her chickens back into the hen house. Never had I heard such squawking, clucking and threatening. When she had finally gotten them all together and on the bus, it took off, disappearing into the darkness with the girls hanging out the windows shouting their undying love and affection for RAF pilots.

We had stayed up late, rehashing the party, so the next morning was pretty rough. Our camp kit and flying gear were loaded on a lorry. We climbed in the back and took off for Setif, about a five-hour ride over a road that was little more than a camel track on the edge of some of the most barren land I have ever seen.

As we rode east, we passed an almost endless stream of Italian and German POW's marching or straggling to the west and prison camp. They were bedraggled, dusty, downcast, and war-weary. The look of hopelessness in their eyes signified their recognition that, for them, it was all over. They had lost. It was now early March, 1943.

Setif was a small encampment on a hill above a dusty landing strip. We were beginning a life under canvas that was to last for a year-and-a-half. There were no buildings, only tents; three cots to a tent, each with mosquito net, and all of one's personal belongings and flying gear. The tents, once occupied by the Luftwaffe, were of heavy canvas, with a fly covering the roof as additional protection from the blazing sun, and believe it or not, snow. The hill we were on was about a thousand feet high, and late one afternoon a freak thunderstorm dumped a good two inches of snow on us.

When I had left home, at my request, a young lady named Betsy, acknowledged to be one of Richmond's most beautiful belles, gave me (and probably a dozen other Romeos) a beautiful formal photograph of herself. Of course, whenever I changed "digs", the photo was the first thing unpacked and placed in a prominent position. Everyone who saw it would drool uncontrollably, not unlike Pavlov's dogs. It elevated my stature a little bit – not much, but a little bit. My quarters soon became a gathering place where they would sit, glass in hand, discussing the attributes of their various female friends and sneaking an occasional glance at my young friend's photo. Of course, I never let it be known that she was really just a friend, nothing more. (I could never have "batted on that wicket.")

In time, Betsy became the Squadron's icon. During our move to Setif her photo was overlooked and remained behind, tacked to the bedroom wall. Such was her fame that its absence was immediately noticed and a "brave" pilot was dispatched in a Hurricane on the 400-mile round trip to Blida. He returned that same day, picture safely in hand, and it was posted this time, not in my quarters, but in the general mess for all to enjoy.

(When I returned to Richmond three years later and tried to present her with her heroic photograph, now oil-stained, streaked with dirt and covered with fly specks, her mother met me at the door and told me Betsy was on her honeymoon with some guy named "Puckett." The name rhymed with my thoughts.)

We were still delivering Hurricanes to the front when our first Spitfire V arrived. The CO suggested that we each give it a go as there were surely going to be more to follow, all requiring delivery. The previous group of ferry pilots who had delivered

Spitfires to Setif had overshot the runway twice, and the ruined remains were still piled up at the far end.

I was excited when my turn came. It's hard to describe the feeling I had that first moment when I entered the cockpit through the small, downward-opening door with the rescue crowbar attached. There everything was, just where I thought it would be: the gear lever over by the right knee, the throttle, mixture control and prop control at the left hand along with the VHF radio. The flap position lever, magneto, starter button, and boost switches were on the instrument panel, and that ever-present, large round compass was between the knees. The smell captured my attention. There's no describing the aroma of hot oil and dope, combined with petrol and superheated metal, all mixed together with the everyday odours of the dust and dirt of Africa. I sat for a few moments trying to soak it all in. This was what I had hoped and worked for, for many months.

The Flight Sergeant standing on the wing broke into my thoughts with: "Just watch the coolant temperatures, Sir, and get off as quickly as possible, or this heat will start her to boiling." I buckled my parachute straps, fastened the Sutton harness, closed the door, gave it three shots of primer with the Kygas, flipped on the mag switches, shouted "Clear," and pressed the starter and booster buttons. The prop turned twice before the engine caught with a belch of flame and smoke, then settled into a soft rumble. A lot had been said about the Spitfire's lack of stability on the ground due to its narrow undercart. Nonsense! It taxied beautifully.

There was little or no wind so we ran it up in the dispersal area. The Spitfire had a long nose and could be easily upset under full throttle on the ground, so it was standard procedure for two erks to sit on the horizontal stabilizer to keep the tail from tip-

ping up during the runup. The mags were checked, and we were
ready to go.

It took to the air beautifully, so light on the controls that it
had a tendency to porpoise as one leaned forward to operate the
undercart retracting lever. It climbed faster than anything I had
ever flown and we were soon level at three thousand feet.

During power-on and power-off stalls, it fell with a slight
shudder just before stalling, as if to announce what it was getting
ready to do. Recovery was simple, and straightforward, with little
or no tendency to spin. With such power and sensitivity at hand,
there was little wonder that my old friend Henshaw chose the
Mark V for his aerobatic demonstrations. After a few rolls and
loops and half loops with a half roll on top, I was feeling rather
proficient. "Overconfident" would be a better choice of words.

Circling our encampment at treetop level to get my mates'
attention, I climbed up to two thousand feet and performed
several of the aforementioned manoeuvres in a creditable manner. I was rather impressed with myself; so much so that when on
the downward side of a loop just above the trees, I noticed that I
had a pretty good turn of speed, and hating to waste it, I pulled
up in a gut-wrenching vertical climb, straight up, and rolled 360
degrees to the right.

Overlooking the natural lag in the airspeed indicator, I noted I
still had 130, decided on a snap roll, and yanked the control
column back to my middle. We went about a half turn, stopped,
and hung there. Everything was quiet; for a moment the engine
quit. I pushed forward, trying to get the nose down. Instead, we
slid backwards and with me holding the elevators in the down
position, flopped over on our back and began a flat spin, inverted
at 2000 feet!

Losing height rapidly, I kicked the opposite rudder and pulled
back to stop the spin. It stopped, but now we were headed

straight down with very little flying speed, and very little altitude. Each time I tried to nurse it out of the dive, it wanted to enter an accelerated stall then flick into a normal spin, and the ground was coming up at an alarming rate. I felt helpless.

The cockpit of the Spitfire Vb.

All that saved me was my pride. I couldn't let this happen in front of this audience, and the thought flashed through my mind that, should I survive, I was going to catch hell for smashing one of His Majesty's Spitfires. I eased it back once more, and to my great relief, the response was positive. The engine burst into life as we made our way over the treetops with me trembling like the leaves of the olive trees in the wake of our passing.

The 'spade grip'.

My performance made for considerable conversation at dinner that evening, not so much about my ability, but about their amazement at what gyrations a Spitfire could undergo and remain in one piece. I never mentioned that the inverted flat spin was not supposed to be part of the act or how glad I was that I had been wearing my brown trousers.

The small town of Setif was five miles down the road. Made up of a few mud huts housing one hundred or so nomadic Arabs and the ever-present bar/restaurant and "cat house," it became our only spot for entertainment at night (the bar, not the cathouse. Heaven only knows what strange diseases might have resulted from contact with those "bits of fluff." Aargh!) We would arrive after dark, drink a few bottles of wine and "feast" on roast goat or camel, and then stagger back to camp, nursing the worst headaches one could imagine.

Glycol, our engine coolant, had a sweetish taste and the Flight Sergeant noticed it was disappearing at an unusual rate. It was discovered that the "wogs", not having access to sugar, were stealing it at night from the maintenance tent and using it to sweeten the rancid wine they were selling in the bar, hence the unusual ferocity of our hangovers.

These Arabs were a strange lot. They would pile three or four foot loads of firewood and camel dung on the backs of their little donkeys and then climb up and seat themselves on top. The poor little beasts could hardly be seen under it all. They often travelled back and forth across the end of the runway heading for Setif or the next little village.

Late one afternoon one of them was leading a donkey with its usual load of fagots, as well as his brother seated on top, when one of our New Zealand allies, Pilot Officer Mathewson, had engine failure; it happened just after he had retracted his wheels on takeoff and he and his Hurricane ploughed right through the little parade. Mathewson was uninjured but the poor donkey and chap on top were killed. The surviving Arab was frightened but unscathed. He showed up the next morning at flight headquarters requesting war reparations, to which he was entitled under British law. His request was for 50 pounds sterling for his donkey and 25 pounds sterling for his brother! An apt example of their lack of regard for human life.

The next week, we were all busy delivering "Spits." I flew one to El Aouina, then one from El Aouina to La Sebala. I got a ride back to Setif with the American Army Air Corps in a B-17. The pilot, Captain West, let me fly it part of the way, and it handled like a truck, proving to me that being a "fighter-boy" was the way to go.

My last ferry trip was partially responsible for a dislike I was developing for the French. The group of so-called Free French pilots who had defected to North Africa when France surrendered, decided to try to reorganize the old World War I Lafayette Escadrille on an airfield next to Bone. Located on the coast about two hundred miles to the northeast, it was only a few miles from the front lines. In order to placate their French "allies," the RAF agreed to equip them with brand new Spitfire Mark VIII's, one of the most advanced fighters being produced at that time and the first to have a retractable tail wheel.

McBride and I each picked one up at Setif and delivered them as requested. We were completely defenceless, as neither aircraft was armed. Nevertheless, our instructions were to get them there as soon as possible. At ground level so as to avoid any contact with the enemy, which at that time included the Italian Air Force, we tore across the desert, just skimming the dunes. We arrived at Bone late in the evening and were met with great ceremony. We enjoyed a couple of bottles of their best wine, and the first real beef steak I had tasted since crossing on the Queen Elizabeth.

We retired early but found it difficult to sleep with all the singing and shouting coming from their mess. Yet one couldn't help but be impressed by their show of enthusiasm for at last being able to join in the fight to liberate their "poor, beloved La Belle France." (I thought if I heard that expression one more time I'd throw up.)

The next day back at Setif, we were told that three of the pilots had defected to France, turned the beautiful brand new VIIIs over to the Germans, and gone home. And here we were, flying ancient Spit V's, risking our necks trying to rid their homeland of the enemy. We were furious! To our great satisfaction, their Squadron was liquidated and never heard from again.

Churchill pays a visit to North Africa in 1943.

19. 253 Squadron, Tunisia

A posting to our first Operational Fighter Squadron came through early one morning. Flight Sergeant Head picked up three of us with our in an old Bisley twin engine bomber and delivered us with all of our equipment to La Sebala No.1 near Tunis. Upon arrival we were so overloaded that he barely managed to bring it to a stop at the very end of the runway. As we were taxiing back, Head admitted he had never flown a Bisley before. Ah, but we were young and proud and we pretended to be cavalier so no one would know we had been scared witless.

The Squadron was named "Hyderabad State Squadron" in honour of the Nizam of Hyderabad, who very generously donated a whole Squadron of twelve aircraft to the RAF. Our encampment was located in an olive grove, with the aircraft and maintenance equipment pushed back beneath the trees, making everything almost invisible from the air.

Things were different on "ops." We had much better food (when we could beat the flies to it). We were still living in tents but the atmosphere was an improvement. The personnel were more cheerful and the CO and Flight Commanders seemed to genuinely care about the welfare of the ground crew as well as the pilots.

About flies and heat: the mess tent, a large marquee, was enclosed in a huge mosquito net and sprayed with DDT before each meal. Regardless, the darned things were so thick, one actually had to brush them off the fork or spoon between the plate and the mouth, and even then it wasn't unusual to get one or two to spit out. Olive trees surrounded the aerodrome and we could see the groups of little urchin beggars sitting in the shade with the damnable things crawling all over their bare arms and legs and probing the corners of their eyes in search of moisture. These children had become so used to them that they had long ago given up brushing them away.

The heat was terrible. In the daytime, even in shade, it would frequently reach 120 degrees. We all wore short sleeved shirts, shorts and sand boots. Bare skin touching metal on the aircraft would receive a nasty burn. Sitting in the cockpit for an hour on "readiness" was such torture, one prayed for a "scramble" in order to cool off.

The signal for "scramble" was a loud klaxon (horn) and a flare shot vertically over those sitting in the aircraft at the end of the runway. We were scrambled in pairs several times to chase Ju-88 fighter bombers that seemed to enjoy pestering the airfields at Bizerta, but by the time we got there, they had been warned and had taken off to the north.

The field was configured as a square, with a squadron located at each corner. With no PSP laid for a runway, the sand and dust was twice as thick as it had been at Blida, so when there was a scramble, everyone on readiness, sometimes as many as six aircraft had to take off line-abreast to keep from being blinded.

Locating a squadron in each corner of the aerodrome was an arrangement that begged for a disaster, and I was almost it. My number two, Flight Sergeant Jack Wooten and I were sitting half-asleep in our cockpits at readiness, when the klaxon went off and the flare went up. The erks had the battery (accumulator) trolley attached, and they leaped to press the power button to give us additional voltage for a quick start. We were supposed to be airborne in a matter of seconds. (This had become a point of pride.) The engines caught immediately and we both started taxiing, as the erks dragged the power cables free. Wooten was twenty feet away from my left wingtip as we opened up with full throttle, and as an experienced number two, he had his eyes fixed on me in order to remain tucked in as closely as possible.

As our wheels were leaving the runway, I glanced to the right and my heart nearly stopped! Two aircraft belonging to the Squadron based in the corner to our right had seen our flare and thought it was for them, and here they came, climbing with noses up and with the proper deflection for all of us to meet at the intersection of the runways. My initial reaction was to duck.

253 Squadron, Tunisia. The CO is right rear.

Trying not to gain an inch of altitude, I retracted the wheels, Wooten following my example, and I held the aircraft down while holding my breath as the two, having seen us, passed overhead. Turning away and scared to death, I had begun our climbing turn when Wooten called, complaining that his engine was running so rough that he would like to abort. I agreed and proceeded on alone, following the vectors given me by the controller. I reached "angels" at twenty thousand feet, only to see two ME 109s disappearing to the north. I reported to control and was instructed to return to base. Back on the ground, the erk's first words, "Cripes, that was bloody close!" described my feelings exactly.

Most of the British fighters were equipped with Rotol wooden propellers constructed of layers of laminated wood, covered with doped linen. I walked over to Wooten's aircraft and realized just how close a call it had been. His propeller was missing about four inches on each blade! This explained his "rough engine." An hour later, there was a call from the other Squadron describing large gashes on the belly of one of their returning Spitfires back near the tail wheel. Poor Wooten had no idea what had happened. His eyes had been glued on my aircraft, as they should have been, and he had missed the whole show. I don't think either of us could have slept that night without our ration of grog.

Yellow jaundice (hepatitis) was our major health problem. At one time, sixty percent of the Squadron was suffering from this strange malady. First the corneas of the eyes turned yellow; then the skin took on a sickly parchment hue and last but not least, one's bowels began to erupt. The officers had three latrines: one for those lucky enough to have escaped, and two for those stricken. It was awful. One didn't dare get more than fifty yards away from a latrine when those terrible cramps started. At first, we thought the yellow Adabrin tablets we were taking to ward off malaria were causing us to turn yellow. When we noticed our stools were chalk white, we knew what we had.

The MO's didn't know much about treatment of jaundice then, so they confined the worst cases among the airmen to a couple of tents. They fed them and us pilots as much sugar as we could eat, but we were never released from flying duties. When it started, I weighed 160 pounds (eleven stone, six), and when I finally recovered from the worst of it six months later, I was down to 127 (nine stone, one). (One British stone equals 14 pounds.) I didn't fully recover for another year. I will never forget those hour-and-a-half long convoy patrols off the coast of Sicily and Malta, suffering with those awful intestinal cramps. If any of the lads had an embarrassing personal accident, on his return he would simply be hosed down by a sympathetic ground crew, with water from the water bowser.

As mentioned earlier, British aircraft didn't have the amenities of American aircraft, such as 'pilot relief tubes' or flooring, so after the new aircraft were delivered, one of the first duties for maintenance was to bore a few holes in the bottom, just below the pilot's seat. A brand new Spit was delivered, which the CO claimed as his own personal machine. He was occupied at the time and asked me to give it its test flight. About half way through I had to go rather urgently and adopted the usual procedure. The CO was waiting when I landed. He had it refuelled and eagerly took off to try out his new acquisition. Ten minutes later he was back on the ground and we had our first and last confrontation. It appears he was so enthralled by the Spit's performance that he attempted a few aerobatics that required a moment or two of inverted flight.

Maintenance had overlooked the hole boring! As he rolled over with the hood closed, the results of my earlier effort, mixed with accumulated sand and dirt, cascaded down on him. He realized what had happened and his next thoughts dwelled on the fact that, in order to right the aircraft, he would have to go through the stuff again. My only defence was, "How was I to know?!" He didn't stay mad for long (about a month), but up to the time I left the squadron, they were still talking about it.

La Sebala was about ten miles north of the city and just west of the beautiful and historical little town of Carthage. On the edge of the Mediterranean, Carthage was cool and clean. It was also the headquarters for General Dwight D. Eisenhower, "Ike," and his Allied Command.

Ike's chauffeur was a beautiful English girl, Captain Kay Summersby. Squadron Leader Ian Bartlett had met her once at a function in Tunis and was in love. The problem was, she was in the American compound, surrounded by American MPs with orders not to admit anyone other than American military personnel. Crafty fellow that he was, he reasoned that, as an American, I could get by the MP's. I had a U.S.A. flash on my uniform and my American driver's license, but I didn't feel it would work. Yet, he insisted and I finally agreed. He telephoned her that afternoon and asked for a dinner date in Tunis.

That evening, Bartlett, Pilot Officer Fred Pawsey and I, deloused, deodorized and dressed to the nines in khaki shirts and shorts, black ties and epaulets denoting our rank, set out for Carthage in the Squadron's one-tonner. We found the front gate, and after convincing the MP of my nationality and answering his many questions as to how I happened to be in the RAF, he became more friendly and agreed to call Captain Summersby.

Kay was a vision to behold. With her raven hair, blue eyes, and dark sunburn, she was beautiful. One could understand why our ginger-haired, freckle-faced CO was enchanted. Kay aimed most of her spirited conversation toward Pawsey because he was Scottish, as were her parents, and to me, to ask all about America. It wasn't long before the CO stopped on the outskirts of Tunis and suggested that he pick us up later at the little bar across the street. That was the last time I saw Kay Summersby, but I really can't blame the Skipper for dumping us; I would have done the same!

One after another, convoy patrols were all pretty much the same. We would circle the ships, the 109's would feint an attack, trying to draw us away so the bombers would have a free shot. A pair of us would peel off to meet them and they would take off to the north. It was sort of stupid. Due to lack of fuel, they couldn't remain long enough to become engaged even if they had wanted to. They still had a certain respect for the old Hurricane. At low altitude, she could hold her own.

It was just as well. Although my records were all in my log book, no one had seemed to notice my lack of gunnery training. I had seldom fired a machine gun from an aircraft, yet here I was on an operational Squadron. At my suggestion, the CO allowed us to practice "shadow firing." One aircraft would fly at 100 feet over the smooth desert sand and the other would fire at its shadow. This was excellent practice for "deflection" shooting.

I awoke one morning with a terrible headache, which was unusual for me unless it had to do with the night before, but recently I had been rather abstemious so it wasn't that. Instead of easing off, it grew worse as the day wore on. The strongest pills the MO gave me failed to bring relief. It reached the point where the pain was so bad that I had trouble seeing. It felt as though someone was poking a red-hot ice pick through my head. It was malaria-like, but called "Sandfly fever"

The batman found me semiconscious in our tent that evening. The doc gave me a shot and shoved me in the "meat wagon." I woke up in Carthage in a clean, cool hospital bed in an all white, tile-floored room with *no flies! And no pain!* My two days in that bed with clean sheets, cool breezes from the sea flowing through the open windows, and three delicious meals a day brought by a pretty nurse were truly heaven.

By the time I returned, we had been reequipped with Spitfire Vc's and preparations were being made to move the Squadron to Italy. It was early September, 1943 and the invasion at Salerno had just begun.

The Mark V Spitfire had a modified air intake for desert operations, but they still had a problem with the sand and dust. One of the erks came up with an idea so brilliant he should have been awarded a medal or at least given a letter of commendation. He covered a small frame with a Kotex-like pad (where he got it wasn't divulged), and attached it to the air intake with a wire leading to the cockpit. One took off, and upon reaching an altitude above the dust level, jerked the wire and the pad fell away. I'm sure the Air Ministry must have been puzzled by the orders from Supply for these things, especially in the numbers that were being requested. (There weren't many WAAFs in the area at the time.) And heaven only knows what the nomads thought when these things came drifting down from the sky!

A problem arose with one of the Sergeant Pilots. He had been overseas for two years and with the Squadron for sixteen months during which time he had flown fifty-two missions. The CO knew that he was having marital problems at home and had never been very keen on flying. He was sent off one day to do a local air test that never took more than thirty minutes, and when he returned an hour and a half later with his fuel almost exhausted, there were some questions asked.

The poor beggar was so emotionally drained that he had become terrified of banking the aircraft more than five degrees, and it had taken him that long to get turned around for a straight in approach for landing. At the Flight Commander's request, I flew as his number one once or twice, and he did quite well. He stuck right on my wing tip during a number of steep turns, steeper than usual, but he was simply unable to do it by himself.

Once again, I saw how harsh British discipline could be. The CO reported the matter, just as it stood, to a group of higher ups who took no notice of the extenuating circumstances, and judged him LMF (lack of moral fibre). He was "cashiered", and thereby condemned to a lifetime in disgrace.

As soon as Italy was invaded, we began covering the convoys off Cap Bon from sunup to sundown. There was little activity on the part of the Jerries as we ground around above the ships. We thought if they were going to contest the landings, this would be the logical place to strike the landing ships, but only two JU 88's ventured into the convey area, and they left as soon as they saw the ships were protected.

Flight Sergeant Freddie Baugh pranged on landing. He was unhurt but his kite was destroyed. He was found thirty feet away still strapped in his seat. Bless that Sutton harness!!

Italy surrendered four days later on September 8th. They didn't have much stomach for continuing, and Hitler's armies were only interested in delaying the Allied advance and saving their own skins. The night before the surrender, German para-troops were dropped on the aerodrome next to us and had the bad luck to be captured immediately by our RAF Regiment.

We had one more trip to Tunis before we had to leave for Salerno, so about a dozen of us got all cleaned up, and headed for town, and the old hotel, La Majestic. It was remarkable how they had managed when the war had been right at their gates. The hotel had been serving and entertaining the German army only a few weeks before, and now the Allies, speaking another language, had taken over. It didn't seem to bother them a bit.

The food was excellent, although it was later confirmed that the "roast beef" had actually been horse meat. The beer, spirits and champagne were plentiful and very reasonably priced. The dining room was beautiful, with large crystal chandeliers and waiters fawning all over the patrons.

Our group, as usual, was rather boisterous, and the American and British foot soldiers weren't much better behaved. There were plenty of unescorted French ladies, in evening dresses, playing hostess to the "brave and gallant warriors," all ready, willing and able to "associate" or just sit and entertain. But we for the moment, believe it or not, were more interested in food.

I felt a need to visit the men's room and took off down the hall in search of one. I found it; a huge white room, tiled from floor to ceiling. Mirrors and washstands lined one wall and mirrors and urinals, the other. Next to the receptacle I was using was the French idea of a toilet. It consisted of a small door-less alcove with a hole in the floor and two elevated ceramic foot prints that were supposed to keep one above it all, I suppose.

The place had been empty when I walked in, and as I stood there enjoying my relief, I sensed that something white had brushed past me and disappeared into that little alcove. Surely it couldn't have been a dress! I leaned over to check and my bladder slammed shut. I must be in the ladies' room! There squatted a pretty young thing with her beautiful white gown hiked up as far as possible and smiling at me as though I was her favourite aunt.

I stood stock still, not knowing where to run, and with no-where to hide. While I contemplated my escape, she emerged. As I stared into the mirror in front of me, she strolled over to the washstands and brushed her hair for a full five minutes. All the while, there I was, holding my "equipment" and frozen to the spot. Finally, she turned and with a smile and a "*merci monsieur*" disappeared through the door. When I got my wits and other things together I headed back to the table. I passed the *Ladies'* and noticed a line of at least ten waiting for the facilities. Obviously my little friend wouldn't or couldn't wait. On my return, I told the story to a rapt audience (with just a little embellishment), and when I had finished, they all rose as one and headed for the "loo."

20. 'Squadron Leader' Smith

I was still on the sick list from my dose of 'sandfly fever' and was astonished when the CO ordered me to take charge of moving the ground party and all the equipment to Salerno. According to 'King's Regulations', being flying personnel I was a "General Duties" Officer. Thus, even though a lowly Pilot Officer, I was superior to the highest ranking non-flying officer. I was "anointed" a temporary, acting, unpaid Squadron Leader and expected to take command. The rest of the pilots were to fly over the Spits that had replaced our clapped-out Hurricanes.

When rain came to this part of the world, which was not very often (I saw rain only three times the entire time I was in Africa) it really poured. It shouldn't be difficult to imagine what a quagmire the aerodrome became. It was flooded. We were ankle deep in mud, our tents were full of water, and it was impossible to move the aircraft without a couple of erks on each wing tip as well as the tail. On the day set for departure the aircraft wouldn't move unless full power was applied which, of course, would set them up on their nose.

The erks came to the rescue. They formed a group of volunteers to sit on the horizontal stabilizer, one on each side of the rudder, until the aircraft, under full throttle, gained enough forward momentum to overcome the drag of the mud. Once it had sufficient speed to keep the tail down on its own, at a signal from the pilot they pushed themselves off, and their own momentum gave them a long slide in the mud. There was some element of risk and there were a few non-serious injuries, but it worked so well that the entire Squadron was airborne within half-an- hour, Once they saw how much fun the first pair had, there was no lack of volunteers. They were flipping coins to see who would be next.

A poor unfortunate from one of the other Squadrons tried to land that same morning, but after he slid about four hundred yards, the mud took charge and over he went.

21. Salerno

After the aircraft left, it took us the rest of the day to pack up all the equipment, fuel the lorries and account for all the bodies to make sure no one was left in Tunis. Extra guards were put on duty that night to prevent anyone from trying for a last visit to the local 'cat house'. We were to depart at sunup, as it was a long drive to the port at Bizerte where our ship was to sail that afternoon.

We made it in time and loaded everything on board an American Naval LST in weather as hot and dusty as I had ever seen. We were drenched with perspiration, hungry, tired and smelly. None of us had had a full bath in months. We cast off just before sunset and hadn't gone a mile before we noticed a dramatic change. We had become so accustomed to the smells of Africa, that the fresh sea air had, to us, a very strange aroma. Nightfall brought sweet relief from the heat; the cool air was a delightful treat.

The American crew treated us like guests at a posh hotel. They immediately led us to the gang showers, gave us soap and clean towels and instructions to bathe as long as we desired in the hot, fresh water. While this was going on, our filthy clothes were collected, laundered and returned to us rough-dried as we stepped out of the showers!

Dinner was served shortly thereafter, and what a meal it was! Thick steaks, fresh salad, real mashed potatoes, huge loaves of fresh bread and *ice cream* – all one could eat. The XO (executive officer), signals officer, intelligence officer and I ate in the wardroom with the Captain. Later, leaning on the rail admiring the star-filled heavens and having a smoke with the Skipper, I noticed he had a trace of a Southern accent. He was from Lynchburg, Virginia, and we had several mutual acquaintances. Small world.

The variety and quantity of food the next morning was as before: fresh scrambled eggs, mounds of crisp bacon, good American coffee and hot rolls with real butter. I hadn't seen such food since the trip over on the *Queen Elizabeth*. Our lads stood up after this breakfast, thanked our hosts, and gave them three of the loudest cheers I've ever heard.

As I congratulated the cook on the bacon (it was Smithfield in cans) and thanked the Skipper for his hospitality, the ship was entering the harbour at Taranto on Italy's south coast. What a scene of devastation: sunken ships everywhere, wrecked landing craft, destroyed docks, and warehouses that had been blown up or burned to the ground.

We off-loaded as quickly as possible and headed due west to Salerno where we were to join our aircraft and pilots, who were being cared for by our sister Squadron, No. 111. It was an awesome trip over southern Italy's most precipitous mountain ranges. The road wasn't really a road, but more like a goat path running along the spine of the mountains. One could see across the valley, little villages clinging to the sheer walls of the cliffs, with only foot paths leading up to them from the valley floor. No wonder there were no attempts at invasion of this area by the Huns. I was amused by the thought of what one of those villagers might say if, after a half-day climb to the top, he remembered he had left his wife's shampoo at the bottom.

We were forced to spend a cold night on a mountain top in front of a fire made in our mess stove to hide the flame. A guard was posted and we had an evening meal of "bully beef" and canned potatoes; quite a comedown from what we had had on the ship. I spent a sleepless night listening to gunfire up North and wondering when we would be in the middle of it. After all, our war was supposed to be in the air, not on the ground.

At first light, I woke up to the smell of bacon frying and, again, the smell of good American coffee. Breakfast was coffee, crisp bacon, and fresh bread, a breakfast courtesy of our American LST friends. They had loaded up our cook just as we were leaving the ship. It was so good, I overate, and not being used to rich food, my stomach rebelled and I lost it an hour later.

22. Montecorvino

This was an abandoned Italian airfield next to the sea. There was really not much more than an airstrip left. The main runways were still pockmarked with bomb craters and useless. I was called on to do an air test the next morning, which didn't take long, and I took some spare time to look around the area. It was certainly different from North Africa. Lush green hills were covered with acre after acre of olive and fruit groves. The beautiful "Med" stretching for miles to the south-western horizon made an unreal setting for the little towns and villages that had been flattened by the fierce fighting of the resisting German armies.

Spitfire Mk IXs were substituted for our Vs, and what a difference! The IXs had more power, a fuel injection system and a two-stage blower (supercharger). While they were heavier and faster and not as much fun to fly, they didn't cut out under negative G as the Vs did. On my first trip, with the CO leading, the supercharger cut in automatically with marked acceleration when we reached 10,000 feet on our way to 20,000. We stooged about for a bit and were vectored on two Ju-88s which we could pick out in the distance, but they saw us or heard us via the German interception radio and took off in cloud to the north.

We were given two "Bogies" at 2000 feet over the coast. The CO rolled over on his back and dropped like a stone, headed on the interception vector. I was right behind when I got the surprise of my life. The blower, sensing the change in altitude pressure, automatically cut out and the deceleration was like hitting a brick wall. None of us had flown this aircraft before and when we returned there was much conversation about the RAF's "on-the-job training."

Two days later, the CO and I took off in formation, and as I selected wheels up, I noticed my airspeed indicator read "zero." Once I was used to an aircraft, I seldom paid attention to the A/S indicator except when on instruments or during a landing. Since I wasn't on instruments, I chose to carry on and finish the patrol and worry about it later. It was the first time I had ever attempted a landing without one but the Spits were so gentle and predictable that I felt there wouldn't be a problem. I came in over the boundary fence, wheels and flaps lowered, and as we lost speed, it gently settled to a perfect landing, perhaps because I was paying a bit more attention than usual.

The Spitfire IX.

The problem was the pitot cover; it was still attached. The Flight Sergeant spotted it right away – a very serious oversight by the erk responsible, but I didn't have the heart to put him on a charge and just told Flight to give him a good "bollocking."

Darn it if the same thing didn't happen again the next day! After takeoff, zero airspeed on the indicator. This time it could have been a bit more serious. We patrolled at 20,000 feet, and the outside temperature was about zero degrees F. After completing our sortie and a rapid descent in formation to circuit altitude, I slid back the canopy. As the warm, moist air met the still freezing cold windscreen, a thick frost formed, making it impossible to see forward. I remained in close formation with my number one, and we landed alongside each other. "Chiefy," the Flight Sergeant, was livid when he saw the pitot cover. I didn't say anything but I understood the two erks responsible were "posted" the next day.

After two more antisubmarine patrols over ships headed into the main harbour of Naples, the Squadron moved to Battapaglia aerodrome on the outskirts of Montecorvino.

23. Battipaglia

Gavin Adams was killed the day we arrived. He just didn't return from a patrol. Gavin, a Canadian, had been a good friend since Hawarden and was one of our group who volunteered for Africa. He and his close chum, Paul Doig, had been inseparable. We never saw one without the other. I heard Paul was so devastated by the news that they had to take the poor chap off flying duties and send him back to Canada.

At Battipaglia we were billeted in an ex-Regia Aeronautica (Italian air forces) training school on the edge of the aerodrome. It was a long, two-story building made of cement, quite cool; best of all, it still had running water. What a relief after Africa. There were no windows and a stairwell went up to an opening in the roof where we spent most of our time when off duty. It offered a spectacular view of the aerodrome, the Sorrentine Peninsula, and Mount Vesuvius, with its spiralling column of smoke.

Watching the different types of aircraft taking off and landing was a great pastime. One strange looking type circled the 'drome twice before it set up on final approach. When it was almost over the boundaries, the RAF Regiment protecting us, opened up with everything they had. They had belatedly discovered it was a Jerry ME 410. It ignored the antiaircraft fire and made a perfect landing.

I rushed down, camera in hand, and took a few photographs as they, with guns drawn, were ushering the pilot out of the cockpit. He said he had thought it was a friendly landing field, and by the time he saw the shells bursting around him, it was too late to abort. The "higher-ups" thought it was wonderful, as this was the newest fighter-bomber Jerry had and the first to be captured in one piece.

We had another bit of excitement the next day when a Beaufighter lost both engines on takeoff and ended up in a heap on top of an embankment at the end of the runway. The pilot and observer hit the ground running just before it burst into flames. The fire was spectacular.

We made several more patrols at 18,000 and 20,000 feet over convoys headed into the harbour at Naples and then a signal came through; we were to move up to Capodicino Aerodrome.

The captured ME 410.

The remains of the Beaufighter.

24. Capodicino

Capodicino, the main airport for Naples, was located very near the base of Mount Vesuvius, within sight of Pompeii and the Bay of Naples.

We were greeted by the most miserable weather we had seen in Italy; rainy and cold and barely fit for flying other than on instruments. There were no paved runways, and the aerodrome had turned into a mud flat.

No sooner had we arrived, when six of us were scrambled to intercept twenty-four 109's to the northwest who apparently were headed to join up with six 109's a few miles to the north. It never happened. They spotted us several thousand feet higher and turned away. Such was the reputation of the Spitfire IX. All we had to do was show up and the enemy would lose their enthusiasm. Unless they could take us by surprise from astern, they didn't want to risk it. Realizing this, made me redouble my caution by keeping my head on a swivel, looking in every direction at all times.

Being blessed with excellent eyesight, and a sense of caution, I was able to spot these beggars occasionally before the rest of the flight. As soon as I would give their position to the leader, he'd turn us in their direction. When they realized they had been spotted, they would scatter.

There were two more unsuccessful scrambles that week and then a patrol starting at sunset. I had never flown a IX at night, and the city of Naples was blacked out when we took off and climbed to 20,000 feet in the darkness.

I was number two and finding it difficult to hold station on the shadowy outline of the other aircraft using only the small riding (formation) light located on the top of his fuselage aft of the canopy. It took a little practice before I was completely comfortable and able to relax and look around. It was slightly overcast, and the flickering flashes of gunfire reflecting on the cloud cover made me realize we were only twenty miles, or five minutes of flying time, from the front.

The Controller was quiet, so we just cruised up and down the edge of Naples harbour, guided by the glow of molten lava oozing from the top of Mount Vesuvius, a magical sight.

It was Christmas Day 1943, and we had been on standby until early evening when the Squadron was told to stand down for our Christmas dinner. We could use it; the rations had been terrible. The cooks had prepared roast chicken and fresh vegetables, and Claude, the head cook, had baked apple tarts, as close as he could get to apple pie, for "the American." The meal was delicious, and as an added treat, the CO produced the long-awaited mail, which had arrived that morning.

I received a bundle of cartons of cigarettes that Dad had mailed months before, with the usual few packs missing. (The postal inspectors always helped themselves but they never took more than one pack from each carton.) Dad had also sent a letter. It had taken the usual circuitous route from the U.S. to Canada to the American Eagle Club in London to North Africa and then to Italy. I didn't have an APO number, and my folks weren't allowed to send mail to anyone not in the American forces, so it had to go through a friend in Canada, Duke Monroe's father, who then forwarded it to England via the Canadian postal service.

On November 10th, my brother, Jimmie, their eldest child, had been reported missing since November 5th and presumed dead.

Serving in the US Naval Air Corps, he had been shot down over
Rabaul while flying off the carrier "Princeton." He had been my
parents' "eyeballs," an excellent student, graduate of VMI (Virginia Military Institute) and a good-looking chap who had never
given them a moment's trouble. I was shocked and I knew how
grief-stricken they were, yet Dad's letter focused on their concern
for my safety, and an attempt to ease my sorrow.

I finished reading the letter and I looked up when I realized
the table conversation had ceased. They had sensed it was bad
news and were waiting to hear. I told them it was about my
brother. As most of them had lost one or more family members,
this was nothing new, but there was an awkward silence and
murmurs of condolence.

I had received the following letter from Jimmie only a few
days before:

Sept. 25th

Dear Park -

*Haven't heard a word from you in several months except
through the family and I understand that you have not received
my last letter which I mailed about six weeks ago. I sent it to
your address in Africa but in the future I shall send them all to
the Eagle Club. I haven't been able to write very frequently for
the past several months because it would have been impossible
to post any mail from where I was. Dad sent me a copy of his
last letter to you in which he mentioned that I was in port in
Frisco - I can't imagine where he got that idea except for the
fact my address has been changed to "Fleet Post Office, San
Fransisco, Calif." - frankly, I have never been within a thousand miles of the place. Of course, I can't mention where I am
but I might say that there is "water, water everywhere and
'nary a drop to drink." I ran into John Towers the other day*

but since he failed to greet me with open arms, I snubbed him completely.

Congratulations on your recent promotion. It was certainly a long time coming but I imagine you will receive the accrued back pay which should be a tidy sum. I can't seem to find anything to do with my money so I send as much home as I can and invest the rest of it (rather unsoundly) in a ship-board enterprise known popularly as "Harlem Dominoes," our sole diversion while at sea. I have seen many a fortune won and lost in a single evening's entertainment.

I was home for a couple of days a few months ago just after the baby was born and of course the house was in an uproar. The entire family and the business now centers around Miss Johnson instead of Winx, who wanders around like a lost soul. Of course they all claim that she is the most beautiful and the healthiest brat ever foaled, but she looked like any other baby I've ever seen. I suppose it will be several months more before she begins to look like anybody. I hope you were sufficiently gratified and impressed by the fact that she was named after you.

Dad and Mother seemed to be in good spirits when I last saw them and Dad's eye continues to improve. His last letter informed me that he made his yearly trip to Hot Springs with "the boys" and played 18 holes of golf and enjoyed himself thoroughly, which sounds good to me. They are all tickled to death with the house and I myself think it is one of the most beautiful places I've seen in Richmond, and the location is ideal — I know you're going to like it. I hope you'll be able to see it before long. I think it would be swell if we could both get home for Xmas but I guess that's too much to hope for. However, I expect to be sent to another squadron within the next few months and it's just possible that it may not have left the States for the com-

but zone at that time which means that I would be sent back to the States to join them. I hope it works out like that anyway.

I was glad to hear that you have applied for transfer to the U.S. forces and hope it will come through in the near future. If the Navy takes you maybe we'll run into each other out there – "quien sabe?"

Can't think of any more news (that the censor would pass) so I'll knock off for now. How's about dropping me a line sometime and letting me know how you are?

Best regards,
Jimmie

Deck of the USN Princeton, Jimmie is 2nd from right, front row.

My initial thought was to let the family know as soon as possible that I had received the letter, and assure them of my safety. There was an American Red Cross headquarters in downtown Naples, and I had heard Americans say they had sent telegrams to the States on numerous occasions. The CO released me for the morning and I located their building, one of the most imposing in the city, and learned how the Red Cross was operating. It was the most disgusting thing I had ever seen. In this war-torn city, among the poorest of the poor, this gang of civilians were living like kings, in luxurious accommodations with food and drink that were not even available in the States. As I walked in, dressed in my uniform as a RAF Flying Officer, I was approached by one of their flunkies and was told I wasn't allowed in the place, that it was for American personnel only. I offered proof of my American citizenship and asked that they send a telegram to my family acknowledging receipt of the letter notifying me of my brother's death. They examined my papers and didn't deny my citizenship, but they said that, as I was in British uniform, nothing could be done and would I please leave. I was furious!

It was a two-hour walk up a hill back to our billets, which were across the street from the main Naples cemetery. There was a constant parade of horse-drawn hearses followed by mourners on foot, weeping and wailing and drinking wine. Thousands of civilians were dying from typhus and there was little the occupying armies could do about it except dust everyone with DDT. It seemed to help, but not very much. It was a very sad sight indeed.

Coincidentally, on the way, I ran into an old friend from Richmond, Lola Thomas, all dressed up in her WAC uniform with Corporal's chevrons on her sleeve. We had only a moment to chat before she had to hurry along to a meeting, and I didn't see her again until after the war.

I almost "bought it" that afternoon. Returning from a sortie, I landed on the muddy grass surface, and while taxiing back to dispersal, I noticed a P-38 attempting to land "wheels up." He hit at least two hundred yards away and began sliding straight at me. I couldn't back away or move forward past the path he was ploughing, so with my heart in my mouth, I sat and watched his approach. The thing was throwing mud in all directions as it passed only a few yards in front of my prop. It was covered in muck, but the pilot's face with its look of horror was clearly visible as he slid by. Another twenty feet closer, and the King would have lost another Spitfire and possibly a pilot.

25. I Join No. 225 Squadron

No. 225, an Army Cooperation Squadron, was located across the Aerodrome. It was manned by a group of pilots trained mostly at No. 41 OTU, several of whom had volunteered for North Africa with me. Tony Golab, Walt Lock, Bruce Evans, Jimmie "Flak" Ward and Dave McBride were among them.

I paid them a visit one afternoon and learned they were operating as far north as Rome, well behind the lines, as tactical and artillery reconnaissance for the Army's 155s (long toms) and naval ships cruising along the coast. Their task was directing gunfire, and spotting troop movements in the Liri Valley and the Pontine Marshes. We had been trained for this type of work at Hawarden. Their casualty rate was high, due mostly to flak from German 88 calibre anti-aircraft guns and their devilish proximity fuses which caused them to explode when the shell came anywhere near its objective.

I had been finding the constant patrols with No. 253 a bit of a bore. All we were doing was grinding around in an empty sky, putting up a show of strength for the Luftwaffe and feeling rather useless. They were short several pilots and their CO accepted my request to join, provided HQ would approve an application for transfer. The posting came through the next day. I had my equipment moved over to their rather elaborate villa perched on top of one of the many hills overlooking Naples. After a rousing "do" in the No. 253 mess the night before, I joined up with the No. 225 on the morning of December 28, 1943.

This villa-living was quite the thing. It was a lovely old mansion with most of the curtains and wall hangings still intact, along with a few pieces of antique furniture and rugs scattered about. The walls and paint were in such good repair, as was the beautiful wood flooring, that it was hard to imagine the place had just been vacated by a retreating German Air Force. (They usually destroyed almost everything as they left, in order to keep it from being used by the advancing Allies. They even went so far as to booby trap the toilets.)

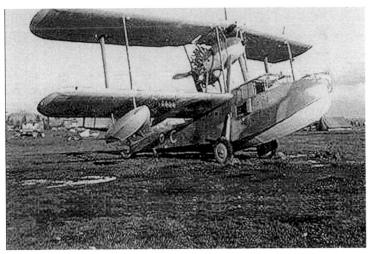

A Walrus flying boat provided air-sea rescue for 225 Squadron.

My arrival coincided with that of a new CO, Lieutenant Colonel Bob Rogers of the South African Air Force, who was to be our Squadron Leader. The Squadron was a real mixed bag of nationalities: lots of Englishmen, three Australians, two New Zealanders, one Chinese, three South Africans, five Canadians, one from Trinidad, one from Bermuda, one part Russian; for a while, a Turk (Turkey wasn't even in the war), a few Scots and an Irishman, Jack Conners (he and I usually flew together).

There were two or three Italian girls, who couldn't speak a word of English, acting as housemaids. My Canadian friend,

McBride had been in the process of teaching them the proper things to say when awakening the officers in the morning. I got my first taste of his efforts when I heard one of them announce, while gently shaking the CO, "Sir, good morning, I would like to ****!" McBride had told them this was English equivalent to "*bongiorno.*"

The Squadron was made up of A and B Flights of six aircraft each, all Spitfire Vbs with their wing tips squared off by removal of about eighteen inches of their elliptical sections. The superchargers were cropped, or inhibited, and as they were older models, they were referred to by the pilots as being "clipped, cropped and clapped." These modifications made for a faster and more nimble performance at or below 5000 feet, where we were to spend most of our time.

We were known as a Tactical Reconnaissance (Tac/R) Squadron. It was our responsibility to make low-level observations of troop and gun movements well behind the enemy lines and direct naval and ground gunfire while circling the gun pits of enemy 88 mm antitank and antiaircraft guns. This was known as Artillery Reconnaissance, or Arty/R. We were instructed not to fire our guns or engage enemy aircraft except in self-defence. It was reasoned that we had to have so much knowledge of our own troop and gun placements in order to properly direct fire, that we would be invaluable to the enemy if shot down.

The day after my arrival, I was briefed and assigned as number two to Alex Milton. We were to penetrate the "bomb line" thirty miles north and do a Tac/R to report on any troop or vehicle movements as well as the intensity of the flak. Locating the flak and reporting its strength became one of our prime functions. Allied bombers that were continually trying to soften up the Krauts entrenched up toward Cassino and the Arno River, were being subjected to heavy losses. If we could locate the gun pits of the enemy's antiaircraft (and antitank) 88's, which could readily be seen from directly above, we could direct the gunfire of our artillery and the naval cruisers offshore in an attempt to clear a flak-free path. The Allied and enemy ground forces were seldom separated by more than five or ten miles and were well within range of our land-based 155 mm's as well as our naval guns which could reach fifteen to twenty miles quite accurately.

Spitfir Vb – clipped, cropped and clapped.

I had been subjected to anti-aircraft fire from some of the convoys when they failed to properly identify our Hurricanes, but the streaks and streamers from their light machine guns were nothing compared to the greeting we received from these 88's. The intensity of fire was incredible. The crafty beggars waited until we flew straight and level for a moment or two and then all fired at once. Fortunately, they were a bit eager and led us more than they should, but those black bursts ahead of us would be close enough to have been set off by their proximity fuses and all explode at once. It was said they could hit you if you flew straight and level, or maintained a constant rate of turn for more than thirty seconds.

It was their practice to locate six or eight gun-pits together with four or five guns in each, all hooked to their main predictor. This allowed one man to aim and fire the lot (about thirty to forty guns) all at once, then they would reload, and fire again. We never flew straight and level for more than a few seconds. Then they got the bright idea of forming an imaginary "cube" in the sky somewhere near our apparent course. As soon as we entered the cube, the whole sky would erupt. Not only would the sounds of the explosions be heard over the engine noise, but also the smell of cordite would filter into the cockpit.

Several of these cubes would be placed in one's path, and as each was entered, the performance would be repeated. One could look astern and see hundreds or as many as thousands of bursts blackening the sky in the space of a few miles. It was rather rattling to realize how many Krauts were trying to kill just the two of us. I have since seen photographs and films of the flak encountered by those on raids to Germany and the rest of Europe, and I can say without hesitation that what we encountered was at least as intensely concentrated.

I have mentioned the naval forces participating in the Arty/R's. This meant we had to practice "shoots" together in order to familiarize them with our procedures. I was called one afternoon to do a shoot in the Bay of Naples with the British cruiser "Oran." It was just outside of the bay and was supposed to fire over the Sorrentine Peninsula at a rock about one hundred feet square, ten miles away.

It wasn't uncommon for the first shot of the Army 155's to be off by three or four hundred yards, requiring numerous adjustments and considerable additional time for us to be over the target. All the while, the enemy 88's would be doing their best to nail us as we circled their position waiting for the "splash" of the projectile. So I was prepared for a long hour and a half (our endurance was only one hour and forty-five minutes with reduced operating revs.)

The ship was steaming at various speeds, constantly changing course taking evasive action, and was subject, as well, to the currents and wave action of the sea. Despite all this, exactly one minute after I gave the order to fire, and was over the position waiting for them to call "splash," there was a tremendous explosion smack in the middle of the rock. Amazing! To prove it wasn't blind luck, I called for a "full salvo" (every gun that could range on the target) and sixty seconds later the rock almost disappeared in the smoke as each shell landed exactly where it should. Think of the technology involved for that kind of accuracy.

I keyed the mike and laughingly reported the "shoot" was over, the target was destroyed. The Skipper came on to invite me for supper aboard ship back in the harbour. I regretfully declined and expressed my congratulations on their fine shooting. He replied that the whole crew was in really top form and anxious to have a go at the real targets up North. One of the lads on a subsequent "shoot" took advantage of such a dinner offer and his description of the meal was not to be forgotten.

The Squadron had been subsisting on British field rations for almost a year: bully beef, spam, hardtack biscuits, tea (lots of tea), canned Brussels sprouts, oleo for butter, canned potatoes, and whatever vegetables could be scrounged locally. One can imagine their envy when they heard the menu the ground crew and I had enjoyed on the LST on the way over from Africa. But, and a *big* but, the American Navy was not allowed to serve alcohol. A gin and tonic or a splash of Scotch would have made that meal fit for a king.

Our Squadron's usual liquor ration had been increased, and as several officers didn't imbibe, we had more than we needed. The surplus was used to barter with the Yanks nearby. They had plenty of cigarettes, orange juice and candies, so all kinds of goodies flowed back and forth. When an ancient but comfortable Lancia touring car appeared one day, and a case of Scotch happened to be missing from the mess, no questions were asked.

I was still flying as number two (known as the "weaver") with Alex Milton. The weaver's task was to fly a weaving pattern above and a few hundred yards behind the leader to protect him from enemy aircraft that might attempt to sneak up from the rear as he concentrated on the troop movements below.

Early one morning as we crossed over the bomb line into hostile territory, we were greeted with the usual enthusiastic gunfire, small arms as well as the large black bursts of the 88's. All at once, as though at a given signal, it ceased. I was new at this (it was only my third trip) and I paid little notice, thinking they may have become tired of wasting all that ammunition. As was my habit, I was constantly turning my head searching the sky for other aircraft, be it a friend with his head in the cockpit, or a foe with malice of intent. I had learned that this simply could not be overdone.

During the lull, Alex had descended several thousand feet in order to get a closer look. Thinking how strangely quiet it was, I looked 90 degrees to starboard and my heart skipped several beats. Here came the answer; two ME 109's not five hundred yards away, headed directly for me. The 88's had ceased fire because they didn't want to shoot down their own aircraft.

Instinctively, I turned directly into them and we passed only a few yards apart with their tracers streaming past my nose. They hadn't spotted Alex, but they were now aware that their plan of "bouncing" (surprising) one lone Spitfire had gone adrift. Jamming the throttle wide open and continuing to circle, climbing all the while to obtain the advantage of height, I called to Alex to warn him and suggested he climb up and give me a hand.

These new 109s had been reported to be far superior to our beat up Mark Vs and it began to show as we circled, one up ahead and the other astern and slightly below. The circle drew tighter and I was beginning to sweat as each of us tried to get enough lead on the other for a deflection shot. I was able to out-climb the one in the rear who was my real problem. His tracers were passing just off and below my wing tip and a maddening thought occurred to me: the beggar was really trying to kill me!

I knew if I could keep him there until Alex came up, things might become more even. I began gaining on the one in front and could see him looking back. Centrifugal forces were coming into play as each of us attempted to tighten the circle. My head and hands were like lead but I didn't dare ease up on the control column. It took a great deal of effort, but I managed to reach the flap lever on the instrument panel and select "down", hoping it would reduce my radius of turn. It did. It confused my "main worry" – the beggar who was doing the shooting, and I was relieved to note that his tracers began to move well outside my turning circle. I think he realized "the worm had turned" when he spotted Alex on his way. One moment he was there, and the next he was gone.

The fellow in front flopped over on his back, headed straight down and turned north over the anti-aircraft gun pits, directly behind his mate. I managed to get off a squirt, but mostly out of frustration. They were at such an extreme range it would have had to be a lucky hit. Alex realized they were hoping to entice us to follow them so their ground forces could have a crack at us and suggested we pack it in and return to base for refuelling.

What a day! One could easily understand a comment Winston Churchill made after having survived an attack during his service in Africa: *"There is nothing more exhilarating than being shot at and missed."*

We had a long chat while we were being refuelled, both of us still excited by the experience of being "jumped." This was the first time it had happened to the squadron since we had been engaged in tactical reconnaissance and we both agreed to keep our heads on a swivel.

Off we went to resume the original sortie and had hardly reached the bomb line when the controller called to report twelve plus bandits over the area. We charged our guns, adjusted our ring sights for the wing span of the ME 109 and climbed as rapidly as possible. We were almost pleased when we noted the efforts of the 88s were as violent as ever, indicating that the bandits had left the area. We were allowed to complete our observations in relative peace. Upon our return, the Intelligence Officer took our report and our explanation for firing our guns, and the rest of the pilots were warned of the increased activity.

Little did we realize the next incident would occur two days later. This time, instead of the Luftwaffe, it was the US Army Air Force. A whole Squadron of P-51s jumped my roommate Tony Golab and shot him down on our side of the lines. He was lucky enough to jump successfully into friendly territory. Tony was a broad-shouldered lad and in his hurry, he actually tore the sides of the cockpit as he escaped. Tony walked back the next day, mad as hell. He identified the culprits, but as far as we knew, nothing was ever done. We didn't even get an apology. Now we knew we had to keep an eye on our "friendly Allies" as well as the Krauts.

Flight Lieutenant York was our Signals Officer; a kind, elderly gentleman, he was always available to lend advice and a sympathetic ear. A few days after I joined the Squadron, having heard about my brother and my attempts to get a message through to the family, he suggested that I write out what I wanted to say and let him try to get through via some connections he had in London. He did just that. Father's next letter acknowledged the arrival of a short cable from London stating I was alive and well, nothing more. That was enough.

Our adjutant, Jimmy Lupton, was perfect for the job. Calm and unflappable in almost any situation, he ran the administrative side of the squadron with utmost efficiency. I never heard him raise his voice or lose his temper. He was the "glue" that held the whole thing together. Commanding officers came and went as did the pilots and ground crew, but he managed to keep things going in a steady fashion throughout its entire operational career. We became good friends and kept in touch with each other until his death a few years ago.

26. Lagos, Italy

Due to the limited range of the Spit, it was decided to construct a landing strip closer to the front lines. It was time to move and begin living under canvas again.

With the exception of a few weeks in Naples, this would make a year-and-a-half that we were to live "outdoors." I more than once blessed the Boy Scout training that enabled me to make the best of what we had in the way of comfort and shelter. One of the pluses was the absence of colds. I don't recall having more than one during the whole period, but it was a pretty bad one. I'm sure I contracted it at the villa in Naples.

Lagos, a little village of no more than one hundred people, was now nothing but a few bombed out apartments and stores. The inhabitants had fled long ago when the Germans pushed through.

PSP had been laid for about 1200 feet as a runway in a small wooded area no more than a few hundred yards from the sea. This was the shortest one we had ever used, and it didn't give much margin in the event one was a little fast on approach. Several times, the much heavier Thunderbolts (P-47s) from a nearby US Squadron attempted to use it, but the pilots changed their minds when they realized how short it really was.

The only place for our campsite was alongside a stream bed that flooded with the slightest rainfall, turning the floor of our tent into a small lake. To my surprise, the nights in "Sunny Italy" were bitterly cold, adding to our misery. The canvas cots were little protection. Our blankets were too small, and attempts to roll up in them left one's arse to freeze below. Golab had the answer; he began saving old copies of the American newspaper, *Stars and Stripes* and used them for insulation between himself and the canvas cot. When word got out, the paper became a very valuable commodity. The resourceful Lock and McBride dug a foundation under their tent, which greatly increased the head-room, and, I might add, the number of visitors. Tony and I, not wishing to lose what little privacy we had, decided against it.

The Author, Lagos Italy 1944.

(A number of years later, Alice and I were in the vicinity of Lagos on our way to Naples and we decided to see if we could find the old aerodrome. It took a while but we found it. A long treeless strip in the woods was the clue. The perforated steel plating used for the runway was long gone, but further searching over toward the stream bed revealed our tent site as well as the foundation that had been dug by Walt and Dave.)

The marquee for the main officer's mess was thirty feet long by fifteen feet wide with a board on two sawhorses for a table, part of which became the bar. Someone had scrounged an old piano, which sat in a corner. The parties started after supper. My "most often number two," Jack Conners, having had nothing to eat but plenty to drink, would seat himself and entertain us with some of the bawdiest songs one could imagine.

Spring mud, Lagos, Italy 1944.

A few of the more industrious souls stacked several empty fuel drums (with the ends removed) up and through the top of the tent, cut a hole in the side of the bottom drum and fired it up. It made a beautiful fireplace but, unfortunately, on the first lighting, the overheated chimney burned off the entire roof. The builders were quite apologetic, had another drink and began reconstruction that same evening; this time with insulation around the roof hole.

Late one evening, I went to visit the canvas-enclosed outdoor loo, and to my astonishment, there was good old Ted, our Aussie Flight Commander, head down, stick in hand, muttering to himself as he stirred about in the dark hole with the aid of a flashlight. I thought that he surely must have lost his mind. Suddenly he stepped back with a cry of joy and held up the stick. On it dangled his false teeth! Apparently, he had been attempting to regurgitate his share of the evening's libations and the bloody things had popped out. I didn't even want to think about how he could ever return them to use. Those Australians were tough!

The Boys of 225 Squadron relaxing; – the Author is 4th from left.

My friend, Jack Conners was a wild Irishman who loved everybody but was very seldom sober. Since he hated flying as much as he did, I'll never know how he managed to get through every day without being killed in a flying accident or by the enemy. I'm sure that thought crossed his mind on many occasions, but being another one of those brave lads, he just carried on anyway. Though full of grog the night before, and having had only a few hours sleep, he would show up without fail for the cold, dark, early morning briefings that were held in the Intelligence Officer's trailer. The British cared little about drinking habits or what one did off-duty as long as one was able to perform his or her duties when called upon. However, heaven help those who could not. They were 'cashiered' immediately.

It was general knowledge that oxygen was a great and immediate cure for a hangover. Unfortunately, it was so frequently used by most of us that a signal came through from Wing Headquarters stating that, due to the unusually high consumption of oxygen by a squadron that seldom flew above three thousand feet, the equipment was to be removed at once.

Connors – in good shape....

Most of us suffering from hangovers had been accustomed to taking a few whiffs while waiting for takeoff at the end of the runway, but Jack had habitually turned his to the "full on" position as soon as he started the engine. As it happened, he had failed to read the Station Routine Orders advising that oxygen would no longer be available, and he had stayed up even later than usual. As we taxied out at first light, along the perimeter track heading for the runway, an aircraft pranged at the far end, and the Controller advised us to shut down, and wait for the tangle to be cleared.

Connors in not such good shape!

As mentioned, the Spit had a little door on the port side allowing easier entry and exit. Realizing we would be there for a while, I unfastened my harness and leaned out for a breath of fresh air. I turned to look behind at Conners and noticed he had opened the little door. He leaned out further and further to wave an acknowledgment. His seat was in the full-up position, and darned if he didn't fall out onto the wing and slide down to the ground. With no oxygen to help, he was so potted that he had forgotten to fasten his harness. To this day, I don't know how he had managed to start the engine and taxi as far as he did.

I climbed out to help and realized he was still 'pissed as a newt'. Something had to be done, and right away. An erk arrived and I explained that Flying Officer Conners was ill and needed help. Making sure he didn't get close enough to smell anything, I sent him off to fetch Flying Officer Bruce Evans, who was on standby. Bruce, suspecting something was amiss, brought Alex with him and Alex took Conners in tow back to his tent. Bruce flew the sortie with me, and as far as we know, the CO was never the wiser.

Conners, realizing that the oxygen game was over, never again overindulged the night before he had to fly; the experience, however, had little effect on his putting down more than a few at all other times. He flew as often as the rest of us, but without that drink, his hands shook so badly at the morning briefings, he could hardly hold the maps. It took a tremendous amount of courage to carry on as he did. I flew more sorties with Jack than any other member of the squadron.

It's hard to forget those dark, predawn hours. The silence would be accentuated by the chirping of crickets and the occasional distant rumble of cannon fire, and then suddenly be shattered by the explosion of a backfire, followed by the throaty roar of all twelve cylinders of a Merlin 50. One after another lit-up, until the sound of all serviceable aircraft melded into a terrific crescendo. The erks loved to take them up to full power, which made the "wakey, wakey" visit from the batman totally unnecessary.

It was time to "take one" into the stream bed, brush teeth, don battledress and Mae West, grab helmet, goggles and oxygen mask and hurry toward the briefing trailer, through trees with leaves soaking wet from the night's rain or early morning dew. It was an exciting start to the day when one was on the roster for the first flight. We never knew what changes had taken place during the night: Had the 88's been relocated? What might they throw at us today? These first flights were the bellwether for the rest of the day and pilots on the roster to fly later paid strict attention to the reports of the early birds.

27. We Lose Alex Milton

January 14th 1944 was indeed a sad day. I had been flying with Dave McBride that afternoon. We landed after having completed a photo reconnaissance but when we were met by a grim-faced ground crew, we knew it had to be bad news … and it was.

Alex had bought it. He had gone off with Tan Ka Hi, alias "Charlie Chan", our Chinese member, and didn't come back. Charlie said they were returning from an artillery shoot and were at 2000 feet when Alex reported that he had smoke in the cockpit, thought he was on fire, and was preparing to bail out.

It was not uncommon for Glycol (the engine coolant) to leak into the exhaust stack where it would vaporize and leave a long trail of white smoke. Charlie told him to hold on a moment, it could hardly be fire because he could see the smoke was white, not black. Alex must have been busy preparing to leave and had disconnected his R/T, because there was no reply.

A conversation that had taken place the evening before made this scenario really weird. We were sitting in the mess after dinner having a few drinks when Alex informed us he had only two more sorties and his tour would be complete. He went on to say how much he hated aerobatics and that he had reached this point without ever having inverted a Spitfire. If he had, he would have known that because of its long nose, when one rolled it on its back, it took a great deal of forward pressure on the control column, or forward trim, to hold the nose up.

The two most accepted methods of leaving the aircraft were to either open the little door and slide off the wing, hoping to miss the tail, or hold the aircraft inverted and drop out. Alex had chosen the latter. He made several attempts before he finally got it inverted, but without forward trim, and being upside down, the nose dropped and the centrifugal force pinned him in the cockpit. Witnesses on the ground reported seeing the pilot struggling to get out. I was sick. This was so needless. Alex had been close enough to the aerodrome to have made it without difficulty, and if he had only once before inverted a Spit...

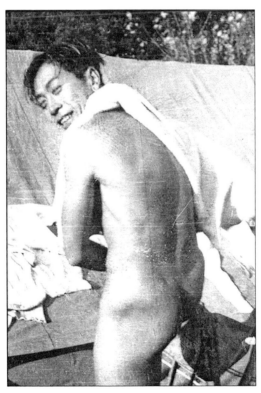

Tan Ka Hi, alias 'Charlie Chan' – our Chinese squadron member; Lagos 1944.

28. Anzio – Operation Shingle

Operation 'Shingle', the invasion at Anzio, started at night on Jan 22nd at 9:00pm. A temporary landing strip of PSP was supposed to be laid by the Sea Bees before dawn. We were to use it for refuelling after we had completed a Tac/R, since the range of the Spit wasn't sufficient to enable us to make it back to the base at Lagos. During refuelling, we were expected to report to the General in charge of the sector to describe enemy troop movements in his area.

Conners and I set off just before dawn on a Tac/R all the way up to Rome, with the hope that the strip at the bridgehead would have been completed by our return after daybreak. The Jerries must have known we were coming. As we worked our way up the Liri Valley toward Rome, the flak from the 88s was the most intense we had ever seen. The skies were black with bursts at our level, both in front and behind, all the way to Rome and down to the bridgehead at Nettuno, the harbour for the Anzio invasion forces.

We arrived overhead about thirty minutes after sunup. What a sight! There were hundreds of ships: LSTs, LCVOPs, LCIs; almost every type of landing craft I had ever seen. Tanks, jeeps, and large trucks rolled down the ramps onto the sand, and what looked like thousands of barrage balloons floated over and around the entire scene. Men covered with equipment were scrambling in the sand among the shell bursts. It looked chaotic.

Conners called out a warning and I immediately banked sharply to starboard just as a Ju-87, followed by two more, passed a hundred yards in front of us, diving vertically into the mess below. They dropped their bombs straight down, then shot back up and raced out to sea. This was one of many nuisance raids, that did little damage, but we were instructed to report only and not to interfere unless we were attacked. It was hard to restrain ourselves. They were an easy target as they pulled out of a dive. (Ju 87s had whistles on their fixed landing gear that made an ear-piercing scream as they picked up vertical speed. One could understand the terror that was felt by civilians during their raids on England, particularly when they took place at night.)

Spitfire Vb and petrol bowser, Lagos 1944.

We located the landing strip, and while it was not completed, it looked long enough for us to have a go, as long as we were extra careful. We made a low, circling "fighter approach" and screeched to a halt at the end, but before we could taxi back, a jeep came careening out to meet us. The manner in which the driver was shouting and waving indicated that something was urgent. We shut down the engines and were climbing out when we heard a noise that sounded like a freight train passing overhead, and then, a tremendous explosion several hundred yards away. It dawned on us why the jeep driver was so exercised. Jerry had gotten the range of the airstrip with his huge 250 mm railway gun, had seen us land, and was trying his luck. We moved... and in a hurry!

This gun was mounted on a railway carriage and was kept hidden in one of the railway tunnels that ran through the foothills along the edge of the Pontine Marshes. It moved out just long enough for a shot and then retreated. This spoiled its aim for pinpoint accuracy, but it continued to play hell with the beachhead. The sound of a shell that size passing overhead was quite impressive.

Before it was finally spotted, we had taken thousands of photographs of the railway line with no success. One of our lads happened to see its barrel just as it was disappearing back into a tunnel, called our Controller with the coordinates, and the fighter-bombers closed it off at both ends. But up to that point, when we made our almost daily landings at the bridgehead, we could expect to be greeted by that jeep and at least one or two rounds from the "Anzio Express." We lost only one aircraft. It was on the ground and unoccupied at the time.

The American General we were to report to, was hidden down in the old catacombs twenty or thirty feet underground. We were escorted by an MP to the entrance which, to our astonishment, was guarded on each side by two enormous "Coke" machines, and mind you, they were still trying to unload ammunition from the ships in the harbour! Well, as they say, "first things first."

We were led through a series of tunnels to the General's office, an indentation carved in the wall, just slightly larger than his desk and chair. This must have been his and his companions' first introduction to a battle area. Conners and I were both embarrassed to note their obvious anxiety about their position, and we tried to avoid looking at the strained expressions on their faces.

We reported the build-up of enemy troops travelling back and forth in the trenches they had dug just beyond the perimeter of the bridgehead. As we turned to go, the General asked, "In your opinion, what do you think we should do?" Conners looked at me and then turned and said, "You're a General and I'm a Flying Officer, but if things were the other way around, I'd bloody well call out the fighter-bombers and in an 'effing' hurry." With that, he saluted smartly, and left me for a moment, standing there with my mouth open. We heard later the General had delayed the request for three hours, and by then, the Krauts having seen us overhead, had dug in and the trenches were empty.

It really wasn't a very good day. When we landed, "Chiefy," the Flight Sergeant in charge of our Flight's maintenance, met us with the news that Flying Officer Robin McCall and Pilot Officer Leith-Hay-Clarke had failed to return from a routine Tac/R.

I had never had the chance to meet Pilot Officer Clarke. He had arrived and put his things in our tent on a morning when Conners and I were on another sortie up to Rome. He had been sent out with one of our more experienced pilots to familiarize him with our operational area. They ran into heavy flak and he disappeared. His kit was still in its bag in our tent. He had been sent out before he had a chance to unpack his bag. Now it was the Adjutant's sad task of inspecting it before it could be sent home.

A Spit from one of the other Squadrons had a problem up at the beachhead and was reported to be unserviceable. Then one of those strange things that occasionally happened during those times took place. The Squadron Engineering Officer, realizing it would take a technician to cure the problem, took it upon himself to commandeer one of the Squadron's aircraft, a Spitfire, and fly it up to the beachhead. He made the repairs and flew back alongside the stranded pilot. Later it was discovered that he not only was not a licensed pilot, but he had *never even soloed an aircraft before.* It took us down a peg, we "brave aces of the air."

I always thought he should have been given one of our highest decorations.[1]

---

[1] The Engineer Officer in question was Greggs Farish of No.72 Squadron, whose remarkable wartime experiences are revealed in full in his book *Algiers to Anzio with 72 & 111 Squadrons* also published by Woodfield.

29. A Beau Gets Two

Early one morning, just before dawn, there was the roar of a single engine aircraft passing just over top of the tents, followed closely behind by another. Next, the eerie, low whistle that identifies a Beaufighter (the Japs called them "whispering death") then the rattle of machine gun and cannon fire. In no time we were all wide awake, and gathered in the mess tent. It was coming on to daylight when we again heard the Beau, this time on final approach. Apparently this radar-equipped night-fighter had chased two 109s over the water in the dark and shot down one at 300 feet but and when he got the other, he had been so low he thought he might have touched the water. When his engines started running rough, he decided to land as soon as possible and Lagos was the nearest aerodrome. I took the photo below after he landed. It plainly shows the tips of all six propeller blades bent back at least three inches.

The Beaufighter - note the bent tips on the propellers.

The daily and sometimes twice-daily sorties up and down the Leri Valley and over the bridgehead, twisting and turning, climbing and diving through the ever-increasing intensity of the antiaircraft bursts, were beginning to show a heavy toll in frazzled nerves and casualties. Added to this was a local US Squadron of P-47's – new, under-trained and something to beware of.

Bruce Evans and I were twenty miles south of Rome in the Liri Valley at 2000 feet when we spotted a formation of six P-47s above us about a mile off our port wing. Recognizing that they were friendly, we paid little attention, then Bruce shouted a warning. The whole bunch had peeled off and were diving straight for us. We had no doubt about their intentions when the lead aircraft opened fire. We tipped up our wings so they could see the roundels indicating we were British Spits and not ME l09s. They paid no attention. We finally turned into them and fired a couple of bursts. The result was almost comical. The whole gaggle turned and dived away under us and disappeared. I guess they realized their mistake.

That same morning we lost Lieutenant Johnny Arryonson and his mate, Lieutenant Theobald, two South African veterans. They were on their way back to base, according to the Controller, when they disappeared over the beach, not leaving a trace. There must have been very intense flak to get them both at the same time, and their loss was a real blow to the Squadron.

(The RAF had some marvellous expressions to ease the impact of a loss. No one ever "crashed," he "pranged." No one was ever "killed"; instead he had "gone for a Burton." Burton was a popular brand of beer. The inference was that he wasn't really gone, just down at the local pub having a beer.)

30. Surprise Meetings & Sad Losses

It was May 1944 when Wing HQ, in all its wisdom, decided to let us stand down for forty-eight hours of R&R, which meant no operational trips for two days. Most of us took advantage of their "generosity", climbed into our old Lancia and took off for Naples. The old touring car had been put in working order and fuelled with 100 octane aircraft petrol by Flying Officer Harry Westbrook, the Squadron's chief scrounger.

There was a beautiful officer's club located on a cliff overlooking the Bay of Naples for the use of Allied officer personnel. What a view! Beautiful blue water, the Isle of Capri with the Sorrentine Peninsula in the background, Mount Vesuvius off to the left towering over the ruins of Pompeii and the setting sun beginning to cast long shadows. We stood there until darkness took over and the scene faded. The area blackout was most effective; there was not a pinpoint of light. We repaired to the bar.

I was dressed in desert khaki shorts and shirt, my rank was shown by my epaulets and RAF wings were on my shirt. I had been with the British almost two years, and like most of the Canadians, I had adopted the English accent. This came about quite naturally and helped to avoid confusion in aerial communications. When I spoke, my accent and expressions had become so British-like that I was no longer taken for a Yank and was frequently asked where my home was in England.

While standing at the bar, having placed an order for a drink, I noticed an American officer nearby, listening to my conversation with the bartender, and frequently glancing at my uniform, and then my face. This continued for a few moments before he finally spoke.

"Are you an American?" he asked.

"Yes," I replied.

"Are you a Virginian?"

Strange, I thought, but replied, "Yes."

"Do you have a brother?" he went on.

This was getting weird, but I told him, "Yes, he was reported missing last November over Rabaul, flying for the Navy."

"Did he go to VMI?"

I replied, "He did."

The next question really surprised me.

"Was his name Jimmie Smith?"

"How did you know?" I asked.

"My name is Marshal Hardy. I was his Brother Rat and room-mate for three years at VMI. If I hadn't had a few drinks and if the resemblance hadn't been so strong, I probably never would have spoken."

We had a drink and a hurried conversation, and then, vowing to catch up later, we returned to our tables. Within ten minutes, an air raid started, and in the dark everyone headed for the shelters. I never saw him again.

Instead of the shelters, we headed for our car, and in an alco-holic daze, sat listening to the occasional piece of shrapnel bounce off the canvas roof. Better safe than sorry, we thought, and decided that under the car would be better. Suddenly it sounded as if the whole world was exploding. We had parked next to two antiaircraft gun pits, and they decided to let go at the same time. One could have read a newspaper by the light of the continuous flashes.

Off in the distance, Mount Vesuvius was adding to the show. Red hot molten lava was flowing over its top and down its sides.

In our inebriated state, it gave the illusion that it had cracked open and was exposing the fiery gates of hell.

When the raid was over, we managed a few hours' sleep, and then headed back to the Squadron just after dawn. Working our way around a bombed out little hamlet, we came to a halt behind two huge US Army trucks and a stalled jeep blocking the road. We waited a moment before trying to pass and, as we sat there, a beautiful, leggy, well-groomed 'WAC' climbed out of the jeep and headed our way. When she was close enough for a thorough inspection, one of the lads let out a gasp and exclaimed, "Jee-zus Ke-rist! It's Marlene Dietrich!" And indeed it was. As a member of a USO troupe, she was on her way to their next gig up at Caserta. She stopped and waved and we, as one, stood and bowed deeply. She was as beautiful in person as she was on the screen and a real treat for us poor female-starved 'aces'.

Two days later we resumed flying and Flying Officer Thompson failed to return. He had been flying number two and, although he was supposed to stay no further behind than three or four hundred yards, his number one had no idea what had happened to him. They were inland at the time, and since no wreckage was ever found it was assumed that he received a direct hit from an 88 and was vaporised. Flying Officer Spencer was hit that same afternoon and bailed out over the bridgehead. He returned the next day, uninjured.

The American Air Force started bombing the German occupied town of Cassino, and as soon as they had reduced it to rubble they went to work on the beautiful old Abbey of Monte Cassino. The Abbey sat on top of a hill at the entrance to the Liri Valley and, reportedly, was the enemy's main observation post. I was sent out with Conners to take low-level photographs of the bombing and its results by flying alongside the Abbey as a Squadron of B 25s unloaded overhead. It was indeed nerve-wracking to fly through the curtain of bombs, which we could clearly see. Concentration on the task at hand was difficult.

We took the photos, and as we headed home, part of the bloody camera came adrift and fell into the control wires in the rear of the aircraft and ruined the film. So back we went that afternoon. Since we no longer had the distraction of the bombers, whatever German troops were left (and there were plenty) were free to make life miserable with their small arms fire. We lucked out, and were given special congratulations on the quality of the photographs (see below).

Cassino Abbey after the bombing, April 1944.

Up to this time, except for an occasional cold sponge bath in one of our little canvas bath tubs, I had not had a real bath since we were on the ship on the way to Taranto. Our laundry was done by any Italian female we could find who would do the job, and we were a smelly mess.

We were overjoyed when a huge American Army mobile shower and laundry trailer arrived one afternoon. An assembly line of hot showers and clothes-washing, similar to that on the ship, began. The whole Squadron lined up before the twelve shower heads, stripped, and threw their clothes into a basket, and then slowly walked through the steaming hot sprays. At the end, we were handed clean, dry towels along with our neatly folded, fresh, clean uniforms. What a treat and how thoughtful of the Yanks! Our CO saw to it that a half dozen bottles of Scotch were loaded into one of the laundry baskets just before they left.

That evening, Sergeant Jimmie Snoxel, head cook and general comedian, produced one of his finest meals. He fried some "monkey meat" (usually eaten just as it came out of the can) in virgin olive oil and threw in a few eggs, tomatoes, onions, and something that might have been cheese and then served it all in a pile. After a few drinks and along with a beer, it really didn't taste too bad, but the next day it sounded so terrible to us that we didn't even want to talk about it. This chap, Jimmie Snoxel, was really a great person. He worked all hours at night supervising the helpers cleaning up the kitchen area and then was out scrounging the next day for whatever fresh vegetables he could find. Up in the dark of early morning, he would brew tea for the English lads, black tea for the Australians, and a bitter chocolate cocoa for the others of us who were slated for the first sortie of the day. *(I have seen Jimmie several times in the past few years at reunions. He is still the same, a little older and, I understand, quite successful. He owns a string of butcher shops.)*

That next morning, Pilot Officer John Pratt was clobbered over the bridgehead, and bailed out. Landing in the trenches of the Allies, he was taken to a local American field hospital with multiple bruises and a sprained ankle. Ignoring his protests, the nurses gave him a bath and a pair of pyjamas and put him to bed. That afternoon an American Colonel made the rounds of the wards passing out American decorations. He didn't identify Johnny as a Limey and Johnny kept his mouth shut and received a USAF Air Medal and a Purple Heart. The Colonel never asked his name or rank – just handed out the medals and went on. By comparison, the RAF and other British forces were rather stingy with their decorations for valour, and Johnny could hardly wait to get back to the Squadron to display his newly acquired "gongs." However, it wasn't to be. The American MO who discharged him the next day, realized the mistake, and a disappointed Pratt was "de-medalled" on the spot.

For a week or ten days the main objective of our Arty/R's was to clear a flak-free lane for the American bombers by destroying the enemy's antiaircraft system along their route. Doing so would allow them to drop their loads more accurately from a lower level. This entailed flying over and around enemy gun pits at two thousand feet, twisting and turning sometimes for an hour or more. We gave them an almost impossible target, but they tried anyway, hoping for a lucky hit.

On the way back from one of these shoots, out of range of their flak and satisfied that we had done a good job, I was relaxed and beginning to enjoy the flight home when suddenly there was a tremendous explosion from the engine. It produced an unusual continuous clatter, and black smoke poured into the cockpit. The prop was barely ticking over, and advancing the throttle had little or no effect. I could see the aerodrome a few miles ahead and felt that I had sufficient altitude to make it if things held together, and got no worse. I abandoned the thought of bailing out while it was still under control and concentrated on stretching the glide as far as possible. The initial rush of adrenaline subsided, as I dropped into the circuit on the downwind leg. My request for a priority landing was granted, and as soon as I was certain I could make it, I lowered the wheels and on a circling final, dropped the flaps and skimmed over the trees at the end of the runway.

They towed me back to the dispersal, and when Chiefy unbuttoned the cowling, he just stood there shaking his head. He showed me a hole the size of a baseball where a push-rod or something had exploded through the side wall. Why the engine didn't seize was a mystery. Had it, the prop would have acted like an air brake and I would never have made it as far as the airfield. A wonderful testimony to the durability of the Merlin.

We continued day after day, directing gun fire from our 155's and offshore naval vessels until a lane five to ten miles wide was cleared well up to and beyond the bridgehead. We were at our most vulnerable during this time. Our practice of never flying without jinking every few seconds may have been the answer to why we escaped. However, they never quit trying. There was always a black puff ahead or behind or alongside.

Our encampment was near enough to the front for us to be able to watch with great satisfaction as the American B-25s, B-26s and B-24s streamed northward through these lanes without the puffs of antiaircraft smoke anywhere near them. On their return, two got careless. We watched and held our breath as they strayed out of the boundaries. A B-26 burst into flames and went straight in and a B-24 above and behind lost three engines and, with several chutes blossoming behind it, crash-landed in the surf within a quarter-mile of our encampment.

A US Captain in their aircraft recovery unit called the CO requesting help recovering the B-24. Being an American and "able to speak their language" I was assigned the task. The Captain arrived in his Jeep followed by a truck containing a Sergeant, about ten privates and a small rubber boat. Off to the beach we went. It was late evening by the time we found the bomber. It was lying half submerged about a hundred yards offshore. The Sergeant and three of the privates rowed me out, trailing a line to attached to the wreck for future trips in case there were bodies to be brought back. It had now become completely dark, but with the aid of flashlights I climbed on the wing and peered down through the canopy into the water-filled cockpit. It was clear enough to see the pilot, still seated at the controls gripping the wheel. His helmet was off and his blond hair waived gently back and forth with the surge of the water.

While examining the scene I commented almost to myself that the first thing to do would be to get the body ashore. I turned to tell the Sergeant and the others and found that I was alone. It seems they heard me mention the "body" and in the dark at that time of night, being superstitious types, they weren't about to stay! The Captain heard me shouting and rowed out to help.

We managed to get the poor soul into the boat and, after assuring ourselves that there were no others, we returned to the beach. We laid the body on its back on a blanket. By this time rigor mortis had set in and it was frozen in a seated position with arms extended as though still flying. I hope this fellow's family got the medal he deserved. Obviously he had remained at the controls long enough for his crew to jump... and paid the price.

Late the next day, my Scottish friend from Hawarden days, Jock McCloud, was shot down flying with 72 Squadron, located on the other side of the field. A typical Scottish lad, he had always been smiling and ready to lend a hand. It was hard to believe he was gone.

On April 21ˢᵗ Bruce Evans and I were returning from the Cassino area and saw Mount Vesuvius erupting. A long, dense plume of smoke and ash was streaming southwest as far as the eye could see. We still had unexposed film remaining in our aerial cameras and the chance of obtaining spectacular photographs was too hard to resist. Mindful of our fast-dwindling fuel, we throttled back to economical cruise, made two low-level passes over the smoking crater, took the photos and just barely made it back to base. The Photo Section made copies for everyone. I still have mine (see below).

Mount Vesuvius - April 21st, 1944.

The photo lads were a hard working bunch. All of the aircraft had vertical and oblique aerial photographic cameras installed in the fuselages. They could be set to take a series of photographs, one right after the other. The results were a continuous overlapping panoramic view of roadways, railroads and gun pits or the general terrain.

Developing and printing a full day of photography by ten or twelve aircraft, frequently kept them working well into the night. Yet, they would still find time to take care of our personal shots, such as those included here.

The next morning I was chatting with the erks as we were walking around the aircraft giving it its pre-flight inspection, when I heard my name called in a voice as though asking a question. I turned, and recognized an old acquaintance, Bob Carlson. Quite taken aback he said, "I read in the *Gazette* [an English magazine that listed all promotions in rank as well as casualties] that you had been killed four months ago in North Africa. You had better write your family as soon as possible."

I wondered how this was possible. I knew there must be numerous "Smiths" in the service, and even if their initials were the same we all had different service numbers. I took his advice and wrote that afternoon. Fortunately, they had never heard about it.

31. Tour Expired

When I joined the RAF, I was filled with the optimism of youth and certain that I would survive. We all felt we were invincible. Now though, after the loss of so many good friends in such a short time, I began entertaining the possibility that I might not be one of the lucky ones.

One night, months after I began flying with 225 Squadron, it was raining hard, and the sound on the canvas roof should have been enough to lull me to sleep. But lying there wide awake, I felt relief that even though I was on the roster, I wouldn't have to fly in the morning because of the inclement weather. I suddenly realized that I was overtired and nervous. I had concern about my personal safety, yes, but most of all I feared not being able to stand up to the pressures and possibly letting down the others.

This feeling lasted throughout the morning briefings, the inspection of the aircraft with Chiefy and the usual banter with the erks. Doing my best to hide my trembling hands while buckling on my 'chute, commenting on how cold it was to those standing around, I climbed into the cockpit and started up. With Conners, as the number two, we lined up on the runway and waited for Control to clear us for takeoff as a pair. The "clear to go" signal was given by the green flare and a smiling Conners gave me a "thumbs up." That did it. If he could still smile with what I knew was gnawing at his insides, I could surely make the best of it. We pushed the throttles wide open until we were tearing down the runway concentrating on the trees at the end, and once we lifted off, and the wheels were retracted, the misgivings vanished. This became the norm: a sleepless night before ops and a feeling of great anxiety, then a calmness as soon as we were in the air cogitating on what lay ahead. I felt better when I learned this was not uncommon among the others. Known as the "operational twitch," we all experienced it, but it was seldom discussed. The tradition was to "press on regardless," and we were expected to do just that.

As of May 15th 1944 I had done 109 operational sorties and was "Tour Expired." I had made it.

I'll never forget those fine young fellows who made up the ground crew, the erks. They were there as we began each flight, helping us climb in, making sure our belts and harnesses were securely fastened, and giving the "thumbs up" sign as we taxied out; and they were the first to greet us upon our return, sliding back the canopy with a worried look and asking, "Was everything all right, Sir?" Hot or cold, rain or shine, they were always there. They and the fitters, riggers, instrument bashers, electronic wallas, batmen, cooks and all the other unsung ground personnel, were the lads who shared the responsibility for whatever success we had.

They worked in the broiling sun, snow, rain, during air raids and sand storms; mostly in the open and from before dawn until after dusk. The serviceability of our aircraft was among the highest in the Wing. All credit to them! God bless them all!

32. R & R in Sorrento

While I was relieved that I had survived, I hated to leave the Squadron and the few good friends who remained. The bright spot was my posting to an RAF rest camp to await transportation to the UK. My mates, Dave McBride, Jim Ward, Walter Lock, and Jake Woolgar would be there as well.

Here was the Italy I had read about, and always wanted to see. Sorrento was a beautiful, small village on a cliff at the tip of the Sorrentine Peninsula overlooking the Bay of Naples. Several miles across the sparkling blue water was the Isle of Capri, probably the best-known island in the Mediterranean.

The "camp" was "La Cocamella," a three-story, family-owned hotel surrounded by an olive grove, lemon trees, grape arbours, and well-kept flower gardens jammed with petunias, all within a five-minute walk to a very popular bar and restaurant called "Joe's Place." The rooms and baths were neat and clean with maid service every day. The dining room and bar offered whisky and wine, and the food was well above the average. There was an orchestra playing dance music at lunch, tea, and dinner, and the local civilian ladies, young and old, never missed an opportunity to mingle on the marble dance floor. It made the war seem miles away.

One of our pilots had disappeared back in January and was presumed dead. He had spent several weeks at Sorrento while on leave and had fallen in love with a pretty little Italian girl named Tatiana Gargiulo, who had given him her photograph. When I left for La Cocamella, the CO gave me the task of returning the photograph and notifying her of his death. I wasn't quite sure how to go about this, having no idea how she would react and feeling the job really belonged to the Padre. However, I asked at the desk if anyone knew her and was told that she was the responsibility of her aunt and uncle, Mr and Mrs Gargiulo. I sighed with relief, thinking that perhaps I could get them to handle it.

They lived on the first floor at the rear of the hotel. As I spoke little or no Italian, I asked the clerk to contact them for me, telling them who I was, and explaining that I spoke only English but would like to meet with them with an interpreter. He disappeared for a few minutes, and then returned with an invitation written in English. It requested that I meet with Mrs Gargiulo for tea at 4 o'clock in their apartments without an interpreter.

Dressed in my best khaki uniform and black necktie, and with shoes shined, I rang their bell at exactly 4 pm.

It was answered by a handsome woman of about fifty years who introduced herself as Mrs Alison Gargiulo, and invited me to come in. She spoke perfect English, and explained that she was an American by birth. Formerly Alison Dix, she had lived her younger life at Westhampton Beach on Long Island. While visiting Sorrento with her parents some years ago, she fell in love with, and married the owner of the hotel, Tatiana's uncle.

We had a delightful conversation about conditions at home as well as in Italy, and I gathered from our discussion that she came from a well-to-do family, but had no way of contacting them due to wartime restrictions. She and her husband were under quite a financial strain, and although she had money in the bank in New York, it was impossible to have any of it transferred to Italy.

I explained my reason for being there and asked her advice as to how I might approach Tatiana with the news of the lad's disappearance and probable death. She suggested that she have Tatiana meet me in the garden at 5 o'clock the next afternoon and that I tell her exactly what I knew. Reminding me of the Italians' strict prohibitions concerning young unmarried ladies, she offered to supply a chaperone. Thanking her for her kindness, and promising to try to contact her family to see if there was anything that could be done to ease her financial strain, I bowed out and left for the bar.

At exactly 5 pm. the next day I stepped out of the side door of the hotel, which opened onto the garden, expecting to see an old crone hovering protectively over a young lady, I was surprised to be greeted instead by an eight-year-old youngster standing by a girl seated under a grape arbour with her back to me. When the little one greeted me, the other, a pretty, sunburned, dark-haired girl in a sleeveless print dress which did nothing to hide the voluptuous figure in a bathing suit beneath it, turned and said in perfect English, "I am Tatiana Gargiulo and this is my chaperone, Carla."

As I stood there with the carefully wrapped photograph under my arm, she stared at me with solemn, unblinking eyes, and I knew that Alison had forewarned her of my mission. I introduced myself and handed her the package. I expressed my sympathy, and gave a brief explanation of the pilot's disappearance. I saluted and turned to leave and suddenly realized there had been no tears.

"Smithy, please wait and sit for a moment," Tatiana said. I looked around and noticed, nervously, that Carla had vanished. We were alone without a chaperone. Noticing my unease she said, "Don't worry, Alison knows we are here and I must explain my connection with your friend. I knew him for less than ten days. He was a nice young man, but he took our friendship to be of a romantic nature. I tried to discourage him as much as I could without hurting his feelings. However, he would have none of it and insisted I give him that photograph. When Alison told me he was missing and probably dead, I was sad, but it would be hypocritical to shed tears when I hardly knew him."

We talked a while longer and when she told me she was out of school for the summer I assumed she meant college. But no, she was talking about high school! Only sixteen, and she had the grace and poise of a woman in her twenties. Later, when I learned what she had been through, I understood.

As I rose to go, she asked if I would join her and her aunt and uncle at the dinner-dance at 7 o'clock the next evening. I hesitated, with the excuse of checking other commitments, knowing full well I would accept. I told her I'd leave a message at the hotel desk first thing in the morning. What was I to do? I was twenty-four years old, in a strange country in the middle of a war, and beguiled by a sixteen-year-old I had known for less than an hour.

Needless to say, I accepted the invitation and found the dinner-dance most enjoyable. Just having the opportunity to talk with Alison – another American – was a treat. Tatiana insisted that we dance and she chatted all the while as though we were old friends. We discussed the progress of the war, my Squadron, and what America had been like when I left home. She was a good conversationalist, asking all the right questions about my family without seeming to pry. Again, I had to ask myself how she could be so sophisticated at such a tender age. I might add that I was conscious of the attention I was receiving from some of my fellow pilots, who happened to be dining at the same time.

The dance ended at about 9 o'clock, and as we were saying goodnight I heard Tatiana ask Alison if she and I might go swimming the following morning. Permission was granted and we agreed to meet in the garden at ten. I headed for the bar and ran into my roommate, "Flak" Ward. He had obviously had a few, as most of us had by that time of night, and was full of questions about the little Italian girl who was with me at dinner.

I tried to slough it off by saying there was nothing to it, that I was merely acting as the CO's messenger delivering the photograph and sad news about her friend.

That night our other roommate got so sloshed he kept me awake half the night calling out in his stupor for his "dear ol' Mom." Thinking he might have a problem, I questioned him about it the next morning. He had no idea what I was talking about; his mother had died when he was three!

33.   A Romantic Interlude

She was there waiting for me, bathing suit in hand. With a big smile, she told me she had something to show me.

The hotel was located on a rock cliff about two hundred feet above the bluest sea one could visualize. The view across the bay seemed to go on forever. A stairway had been carved inside the rock and wound down and around with an occasional window providing some light, but not much; I followed Tatiana down to a smooth, black sand beach made of Vesuvius' lava that had been pulverized by the sea.

We swam until well after lunchtime. The salty water was so buoyant that swimming was effortless and we ventured well beyond a safe distance from the beach. Tatiana swam like a fish. We were both in good physical condition and not in the least tired, when she suggested we take a look at what she wanted to show me.

We swam up to a sheer rock wall and she called, "Follow me!" and dove right at the rock and disappeared. I hesitated a moment but when she failed to reappear, I followed. Swimming under water beneath a rock is not a fun pastime. After about sixty feet, I was getting a little panicky and wondering what I had gotten myself into, but then I noticed the clear water ahead was brightening. I broke the surface, gasping for breath, to the sound of her laughter. In the muted light, I could see her sitting on a ledge dangling her feet in the water and making fun of my frightened expression.

We were in a grotto, a cavern lit by daylight filtered through the water from the opening. The entrance became invisible only at high water and, being familiar with the tides, Tatiana had waited until that moment for us to enter. Had it not been so fascinating and beautiful I might have strangled her on the spot. We laughed about it, but I insisted on waiting until the tide receded enough for us to return to daylight and open air.

Lolling on the beach and swimming for hours on end became a daily routine. I would emerge from an early morning breakfast and she would be there in the garden twirling her bathing suit. With a "*bon giorno*" and a big smile she'd ask, "Would you like to swim today?" It didn't require an answer and off we'd go.

As I mentioned, Alison and her parents in the States were apparently quite wealthy, but she had been unable to obtain funds from her bank in New York. We discussed this one day and worked out a plan that proved to be a big help. I had little use for money while in Italy so I gave her about three quarters of the pay I hadn't drawn, about a thousand dollars in lira, and she wrote me a check on her New York bank. I sent the check to Dad with a note of explanation and he deposited it in my account at home. This was done on several occasions without mishap, and I was well rewarded with a very touching letter from her many months after my return to England.

Alison and Tatiana wanted to show me the town of Sorrento as the Italians knew it, and also do a little shopping. I "requisitioned" the Lancia, piled them in along with Carla, and off we went. I think the town is still talking about it.

The darned car would go about a hundred yards, jerk, backfire, and go another hundred if we were on level ground or headed downhill. Going uphill was another matter. Due to an unruly fuel pump and the effects of gravity, it would just quit. It dawned on us that if it worked facing downhill, the solution would be to back it uphill. This worked fine except for the problem of steering while in reverse, and the comments in Italian from the pedestrians. Tatiana wouldn't tell me what they were saying. Fortunately, once we arrived in the town, the streets were level and we got about quite nicely. We learned to live with the explosions and the stares.

Tatiana's father owned and operated a very successful and famous woodworking shop that specialized in inlay work. He was absent and I never did meet him, but one of his artists showed me several examples of their work, including a magnificent inlaid baby grand piano that had taken first prize at the Chicago World's fair.

One could tell from the bowing and scraping that the Gargiulo family was well-known and respected, even though Tatiana's mother had left with a German officer when they retreated to Rome. Tatiana had no idea where she was.

The Italians on the whole were pleased to see us as their "liberators" and treated us accordingly. They had never really had their hearts in the war, and most felt that Mussolini had sold them a bill of goods when he allied them with Hitler. They were fun-loving and easygoing, and though poor by our standards, they seemed happy with their lot.

I usually spent the evenings, when Tatiana was unable to escape her nine o'clock curfew, with McBride, Lock, Ward and Woolgar (when the latter was not "seeing snakes") at our beautiful little cafe that was not so far from the hotel that we couldn't get home under our own steam. It had a veranda that hung over the top of the cliff with a view over the darkened Bay of Naples. We would sit there for hours, drinking "Lacrima de Christi," a very good local wine, telling war stories and baring our souls.

After one such evening, we were pretty well in our cups but managed to find our way home, and to our room on the second floor. I was almost asleep (or passed out) when it came to me that McBride had one leg over the window sill and was struggling to get the other over. "Mac," I asked, "What the hell are you doing?" "Gonna take a leak." was the response. We told him, "You Dummy, it's twenty feet down," and with that, we retrieved him and held him at the window while he watered the terrace below. (At our first postwar meeting fifty years later, he recalled the incident and thanked me "for saving his life". He said he had thought that first step was pretty high!)

Two weeks of good food, good wine, soaking up sunshine and swimming with a charming young lady for hours on end each day worked wonders on my morale, and I was ready to resume my responsibilities. Transportation back to the UK would be taking place any day now. Ordinarily, I would have looked forward to getting back but I had begun to realize with a sinking feeling that I had become emotionally involved with my little Italian friend and was going to find it hard to say good bye.

This was solved, perhaps not to my satisfaction, by the arrival of a lorry at 5am bearing instructions for our departure by air in one-half hour. We were limited to a baggage allowance of only twenty pounds plus our flying gear, so it didn't take long to pack. I was at the front desk at 5:15. Having paid my mess bill, I turned to leave, and there she stood. I have no idea how she knew (their intelligence gathering was probably better than the Allies') but she and Bruce Evans' friend, Anna Nicolini, had come to say goodbye. Without going into details, the ensuing scene gave our fellow pilots plenty to rag us about for the entire trip back to "Old Blighty".

34. Return to England

Our transportation was an old, tired Wellington with bucket seats lining each side, indicating it had been used to carry passengers instead of bombs.

The flight back was non-stop, at night, over the Italian Alps, across parts of Southern France, then over the English Channel and into Hendon, just outside London, all without fighter escort. I was a little apprehensive, having been frightened in the past by experiences with pilots of unknown ability, particularly ferry pilots, who frequently had little or no previous time on the aircraft they were asked to fly. It was a moonlit night, and one could just make out the tops of the snow-covered Alps as the old "Wimpy" strained for altitude.

Then it happened. The sound of both engines sputtered, then ceased simultaneously, followed by a thundering silence. We were all sitting on our 'chutes, and for a moment, paralyzed. Suddenly we were galvanized into action, and there was a mad scramble by everyone to get the things on and head for an exit. (There wasn't any except the bomb bay.) As quickly as they had quit, both engines restarted when the co-pilot switched to auxiliary tanks. The silly clots had let the main tanks run dry. The language and death threats from the passengers were awesome.

A beautiful sunrise ushering in a warm spring day greeted us as we arrived. It was good to be back in the land of "bubble and squeak." A small lorry driven by a pretty little WAAF was waiting for "Flight Lieutenant" Smith with instructions to transport me immediately to London. This was strange. The others were going on leave for a month but I was to report to the RAF Air Officer

Commanding (AOC) in Whitehall, obviously for further posting.

Dirty, smelly, and unshaven, I was ushered into his office, still carrying my kit bag. He paid little notice and asked that I take a seat, saying he wanted to ask me a few questions. He danced around for a while, asking about my Italian experience, and why I hadn't transferred to the U.S. forces, and made other small talk. I was getting more uneasy by the minute, afraid I would be sent home or grounded from flying duties and given some menial desk job.

Finally he got to it. They were desperately short of instructors at Hawarden's No. 41 OTU and needed someone with operational experience on Spits and Hurricanes and flight time on AT 6's and P-51's. My flying records indicated I was a prime candidate, except that I was entitled to a month's leave, and they needed me now, but it had to be voluntary. I tried to hide a smile. I had no idea where I would go, or what I would do, on leave by myself for a month. The others had homes or relatives or sweethearts, and I would be completely alone. I'd much rather be on a good station or back on a Squadron.

I feigned disappointment, but agreed if he would see to it that I was posted to an operational P-51 Fighter Squadron at the end of the six-month instructing period. He was happy to accept my proposition. I couldn't believe it. Here I was, bargaining with an AOC ! Six months later, almost to the day, he kept his part of the agreement.

I stepped outside to an unchanged London except for a reduced frequency in the air raids. However, people still spent as much time as before, looking skyward. This time, looking for "Buzz Bombs."

Food in London was not as scarce as it had been. A lot of the population had fled to rural areas to escape the sleepless nights.

This left most restaurants, still on a ration system, with an increase in the available food supply. An Indian restaurant off Piccadilly, "Veeraswami" was one of the best, offering all types of curry with the accompanying spices as well as fresh seafood, chicken, beef, and lamb served by pretty young Indian girls and tall, turbaned Indian men. (It was still in business at the same location when Alice and I were in London, fifty years later.) I spent the afternoon in the pub at the Regent Palace Hotel, the evening eating the biggest serving of curry they had at "Veeraswami," and the night at the American Eagle Club.

35. Back to RAF Hawarden

Training Command stations were, by this time, pretty well off as far as food and accommodations were concerned. Permanent Staff (and I was now considered to be among those) had especially comfortable quarters as well as a large staff of servant personnel. Each instructor had a single room with bed, bureau, chair, and iron stove for heat (with those three lumps of coal). A batwoman was shared by two officers; real luxury when one considers how I had been living for the past eighteen months.

One of the batwomen's duties was to make sure we were awakened at the proper hour with hot tea, warm water, and a stove lit with those three lumps of coal. The fire took off the chill and lasted only long enough for one to wash and dress hastily. From spring until late summer, the weather was delightful, but fall and winter in those Welsh hills were bitter. One morning in early December, we woke to frozen water pipes all over the entire station. They remained so for the better part of a week. What a mess!

It took spunk for these young women to endure such hardship. They were up at four or five a.m. in the frosty mornings, frequently in snow, lugging those buckets of hot water and the lumps of coal. They shined our shoes, pressed our uniforms, polished our buttons, and took care of the laundry and sewing-on of buttons and the thousand other things that made life more comfortable. I hope they realize how much their efforts were appreciated.

There must have been at least 2000 non-flying personnel on the station; fitters, riggers, instrument bashers, wireless operators, weather wizards, tower operators and controllers, administration and headquarters people, cooks and cleaners, all working together with overall responsibility for keeping the aircraft serviceable and the pilots fit, fed and flying. They did a superb job. Having been promoted to Flight Lieutenant with two years' seniority and, being an American "Volunteer Reserve" as opposed to "Regular" RAF, I seemed to get more attention than I deserved.

Hurricanes in the snow - Hawarden '43- *painting by Wooten.*

During the cold winter months, the airmen and airwomen on the field were more than heroic. They were pushing freezing metal aircraft from one position to the next without gloves, using their woollen mufflers to cover their hands, leaving their chests and throats bare to the elements. Strictly against orders, we began to let them borrow our fur-lined flying gloves which were duly returned each evening. I am certain the Wing Commander in charge of flying was aware of what was going on, but it was never mentioned.

The station Padre was responsible for distributing to all ground crew, the gloves and scarves made available, in very limited quantities, by "Bundles for Britain" and the Red Cross. I approached the Padre in the mess after one particularly bitter day, and when I pointed out their misery, I was told that the supply of these "luxury" items was exhausted. It was discovered a few weeks later that the bloody sod had been flogging most of the donated equipment for a tidy sum to some civilians in Chester. He was "cashiered" immediately and, I hope, ended up in jail.

Walking or cycling down the two miles to Flights each day, I passed Headquarters, with its RAF and British ensigns flying, and the enormous maintenance hangars filled with the hustle and bustle of aircraft being refuelled or repaired. Engines roared as they were run-up. Passing airmen and WAAFs saluted. It made an impression. I felt a sense of satisfaction having become a commissioned officer, and a pilot, flying Hurricanes, Spitfires, P-51s and Harvards (AT 6s) – aircraft I would never have dreamed of flying a few years ago. It made me feel as though now I was really a part of the total effort.

The Station Commander, a Group Captain, was a very unpleasant little tyrant and a sadist if ever there was one. He had a big English bulldog that hated cats. His favourite sport was to stroll around the station with the dog on a leash and hunt for one of the many scrawny cats that inhabited the area hoping for a handout or a stray mouse. When one was spotted, he'd release the dog, urge him on and cheer when he crushed one of the unfortunates in his powerful jaws.

Squadron Leader Grey happened to like cats and one afternoon was "privileged" to see one of these gruesome performances. A few days later he saw the dog unattended out-side the CO's office, grabbed him by the scruff of the neck, and began to strangle him. The dog passed out and was lying on the ground with Grey on his knees, hands still around its throat when the CO rounded the corner.

"Oh, Sir," said Grey, "Something seems to be wrong with your dog and I'm trying to revive him." About then, the dog regained consciousness, opened one eye, saw its tormenter, leaped to its feet, and took off like a shot. Although the incident was wit-nessed by a group of bystanders, much to their credit, the Group Captain was never made the wiser. He did, however, remain a vindictive little sod.

One night after dinner, a few of us were standing around the bar in the mess when one of the more attractive WAAFs on the station, Section Officer Fair, announced that there was a station dance for all ranks taking place that night at 8 o'clock in the main hangar. This didn't seem to be of any particular interest to those present, so we ordered another round of drinks, and con-tinued our conversation.

By 9:00, the others had all drifted off, leaving Section Officer Fair and me standing in front of the open fire, downing another. She again brought up the subject of the dance, saying that the Group Captain had asked her to go with him, but she couldn't stand the idea and had told him she had a headache.

"Come on, Smithy, let's go."

"Frances, suppose he's there?"

"Then I'll tell him I took an aspirin," she responded.

Having gone through several pints of 'arf and 'arf and not wishing to disappoint a lady, I was easily persuaded. Off we went in the pitch black night down to the hangar and, as luck would have it, the first person we ran into in the brilliantly lit entrance was the Groupie. He was with some poor unfortunate little twit but he spied us immediately, and with his measly little moustache all a twitter, he started in our direction. She hurried toward him, met him halfway, and I heard her say, "Oh Sir, I felt so much better, and when I ran into Flight Lieutenant Smith, I asked him to bring me down to find you, and I hoped I wouldn't be too late. But I see you found someone else, so I'll get him to take me back to the Castle." (The Castle was the WAAF officers' sleeping quarters.) I could tell from the look he gave me that he didn't believe a word of it, but there was little he could do or say in front of his date.

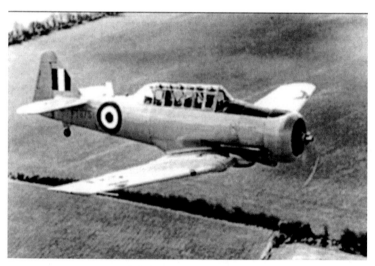

Harvard flight trainer – Hawarden 1944.

Being full of grog, we couldn't have cared less. We stayed a good while longer and enjoyed the opportunity of mixing with the lower ranks, then headed for the Castle in the dark of the blackout. We stumbled and fumbled our way up the hill to the entrance of the old stone building. By now a wet snow was falling in earnest, the wind had gotten up, and it was cold as hell.

The icy blasts penetrated our greatcoats and we were both wet and shivering. There wasn't a sound or a pinpoint of light from inside when she suggested we go in and build a fire in her "little room" to dry out, and get warm with a small glass of scotch.

No one will believe this… This "hen coop" contained nothing but female officers and was supposed to be off-limits to all male personnel. I knew how much our little friend, the Groupie, would delight in a report that his "favourite" Flight Lieutenant had been caught with his you-know-what where it shouldn't be, so I made one of the toughest and perhaps wisest decisions I had ever made for King and country. I saluted and maybe even kissed her, but without responding to her suggestion, began that long, cold walk back to my "little room" a mile down the hill, kicking myself all the way.

Unbeknownst to me, this had been a very dangerous game, as I learned several months later. She had failed to tell me that the CO had a "thing" for her from the first day she arrived on the station. Oh my! We have a saying back home in Virginia: "A wise monkey don't never monkey with another monkey's monkey." I should have remembered it. I didn't need an enemy as my Commanding Officer.

My cohorts and good "partners-in-crime" were ex-operational pilots who, having completed their tours, were relieved and obviously relaxed. Now that they had left the war behind, all they had left to do was survive being instructors and that darn Group Captain. It wasn't easy, and I never heard if they did.

36. RAF Poulton

The airdrome at Hawarden was becoming a bit crowded, particularly at "tea time." Old habits are hard to break. It was now as it had been two years before. Afternoon Tea was at 4:00. At 3:30 the circuit would be jammed with aircraft, a stream of sometimes fifteen or twenty on the downwind leg at the same time. This would include several Wellington and Lancaster heavy bombers from the maintenance unit across the aerodrome, all jockeying for a priority for landing. Some were even known to cheat by declaring a petrol shortage, which gave them immediate landing rights. Everyone was always half-starved, so I guess we had good reason not to miss tea.

This was putting such a strain on the Hawarden facility that the higher ups decided to open a satellite field twenty miles away, known as "Poulton," a group of Nissen huts surrounded by a sea of mud. But we who were stationed there loved it for its lack of "bull." The Administration all stayed at Hawarden, and we ran the Poulton show without interference, and except for an occasional visit from the senior staff, were undisturbed.

There were six officers to each Nissen hut. These were made of a half-round piece of corrugated metal pipe twenty feet in diameter. Each had a concrete floor, doors and windows at each end, and an iron stove in the centre, all in one big room with no partitions. Outside about ten feet away was another, half the size, sunken in the ground and covered with sod, which served as our air raid shelter.

Poulton had once been a large dairy farm, and the rich earth covering the shelter produced the largest and most delicious crop of mushrooms I had ever seen. We would step out the door on the way to early breakfast, pluck one the size of one's hand, and give it to the cook as we walked in. As we finished our porridge, we would be presented with a broiled mushroom crowned with a slice of tomato and a fried egg, all on a slice of fried bread. We were rationed to two eggs a week, but the mushrooms were just as delicious without them.

LACW, Mary Thomas, our batwoman - Poulton 1944.

I had been there ten days when a posting came through, sending me to No. 3 Flying Instructors' School at Lulsgate Bottom, down in South-western England. Nearby was the Cheddar Gorge, home of the world-famous cheddar cheese. The course was to take five weeks.

The night before leaving, I was in the bar having one with Alex Milne, an old friend from previous Hawarden days, when I noticed his eyes. The whites were as yellow as a canary. In the desert, this was a sign of yellow jaundice and not uncommon. I mentioned it, and he said he felt fine, but when he looked in a mirror on the way out, he agreed to see the MO the next morning. Two weeks later they called me at Lulsgate to tell me he had been sent to the hospital where they had operated on his liver. He had died on the operating table.

Flight Lieutenant Ian "Chiefy" Cauldwell, a Canadian who was white but had the features of an American Indian, flew me down to Lulsgate in a Harvard. He was one of the group who had volunteered to go with us to Africa almost two years before. He stayed long enough to have a beer, and we walked down to Flights together. He looked worn-out, and with a touch of the operational twitch. I watched him take off. It was the last time I saw him alive.

He was flying over the aerodrome at Hawarden a week later in an overcast with a thousand-foot ceiling, when those on the ground saw his aircraft, engine screaming, break through the cloud cover in a vertical dive. It went straight in, leaving nothing but a smoking crater on the edge of the aerodrome near A Flight's hut. Declaring they had never seen a crash and despite being warned by the Flight Commander, several WAAFs headed for the site. They returned several moments later, white, weeping and vomiting. Parts of Ian's remains were in a tree. The investigators never found the cause of the crash, and there wasn't enough left for an autopsy.

Poor Chiefy. He and his girl Chappie were to be married the following month. She, only a Lieutenant Canadian Army nursing sister, stormed into the Group Captain's office unannounced, and in rather pithy language, blamed him for allowing Ian to fly when he was in such poor shape. She had a good point. Ian had been in the RCAF for a longer time than most pilots his age, and had certainly done his share of operational flying, target towing and instructing, but like so many of those lads, they had to be told when to quit.

37. RAF Lulsgate Bottom

The aerodrome was located about three miles from the town of Lulsgate that consisted of a church, a pub, and a few thatch-roofed houses. The pub, of course, was the hub of social life, particularly at night. Nothing like the pubs of today, the bar was divided into two sections, one for ladies and one for gentlemen, who at the time were all elderly, the young having gone to war. The ladies sat in what resembled pews facing the men, who sat on stools at the bar. Everyone talked at once and sang and smoked as though there would be no tomorrow. I always had a pack of American cigarettes that I placed on the bar, and gladly shared with all present including the women.

These people couldn't have been more kind to us – me especially – after one of the lads let it be known that I was "the American". None of us was allowed to pay for the many pints we consumed or the occasional "wee dram" of spirits – in such short supply it was kept hidden under the bar and reserved for very special patrons. We would, however, leave a healthy tip for the publican before we staggered out into the dark night to stumble our way home. We learned that our bill had been covered by voluntary contributions from the barkeep and the farmers, despite their modest means.

We experienced this type of gratitude almost everywhere we went, and at times it was almost embarrassing. We felt we might be thought of as freeloaders and after much insistence we were occasionally allowed to buy a round for all those present.

Wing Commander Barney Berrisford (later known as Sir Barney) was CO at Lulsgate; he was one of the finest I had throughout my career with the RAF.

Our training was given in the old Miles Master II, one of the first British aircraft I flew at Tern Hill. At that time, I didn't appreciate the trials and tribulations of the poor instructors, but this time *I* was in the rear (instructor's) seat. I have previously described the huge forward cockpit and the lack of visibility over that enormous Bristol engine. The instructor's cockpit ("office" as it was called) was tiny and the forward visibility was zero when on the ground in a three-point attitude or in the air on final approach. The solution was a barber-chair-like post on which the rear seat was mounted, and a hinged, clear plastic canopy – not unlike a clam shell – over the top of the cockpit.

On takeoffs or landing when the airspeed was reduced, the instructor would reach up, pull a handle to hinge the canopy open to a clamshell position, then reach down and pull a lever that would elevate the seat until the poor chap's head was almost in the slipstream. Afforded little protection from the 120 mile-per-hour wind and noise, his eyes watering behind his goggles, he would do his best to see what the student was doing that might possibly kill them both. This was bad enough in good weather, but at night or in the frigid winter rain and fog, it was almost intolerable. All of this time, the instructor was supposed to be calmly giving the student instructions or words of caution.

Night flying was a terror. Sitting in that elevated seat trying to locate those tiny runway lights with tears in ones eyes (from wind or agony, we couldn't tell) was an experience I'd like to forget. I still wonder if there were as many fatalities in Training Command as on the Operational Squadrons.

I completed the course, had my check ride with the Wing Commander, and got his signature in my log book, testifying that I was an "above average pilot" and a "Certified Flight Instructor," a dubious honour at best. I was waiting for transport back to Hawarden when a signal came through from London. Mrs Dexter at the American Eagle Club had a very urgent message for me...

38. A Miracle Cure

The message concerned a Sergeant Christian, who was on his deathbed and asking for me. I knew several people named Christian but couldn't imagine which one this could be or how to get in contact. Was he British or American? Mrs Dexter had said the only clue she had was that he had told his doctors that I was his neighbour, but failed to say whether in England or America.

I puzzled over this until the next day and then called her back. She then remembered that they had told her he was in an American Field Hospital in the Salisbury Plains. That settled it. It had to be either Andy Christian or Stuart Christian, although I hadn't been aware that either was in this part of the world.

I went to the CO, told him the problem and asked if he could suggest any way I might locate this Sergeant Christian. He didn't hesitate, saying, "The Salisbury Plains are smooth, rolling hills with no trees or hedgerows. Take my Magister, fly over, and when you see a big marquee with a red cross on the top, land alongside. Those hospitals are all over the place." I accepted his generous offer and was airborne in the little low-wing, open-cockpit, two-seater within the hour. It was a beautiful day, and from a thousand feet one could see several of these enormous "circus tents" with a large red cross on top. But which one held the Sergeant?

I landed beside the first one I came to, but they had no idea where he might be, and were not permitted to give out any information to anyone not in the American forces because "Christian was a battle casualty." It was useless to argue so I took off to resume my search. There was another marquee on the outskirts of Upavon, and on top of a hill next to it was an RAF airfield. I landed to refuel and hitched a ride over to the hospital.

I was met by the Adjutant, a Second Lieutenant, who pored over his records for a few minutes. I was about to turn and leave when he acknowledged that there was indeed a Sergeant Stuart Christian in the intensive sick bay. I told him that he was my friend and that I would like to see him. "Can't be done," he said, "He is a battle casualty and you are in a foreign service." I was as nice as could be at first, explaining that I had proof that I was an American, that we were neighbours in Richmond, and he had asked to see me. He wasn't moved and ended the interview by rudely turning his back. I was about to explode, saying that I had looked all over the Plains for Christian and wasn't about to be denied seeing him by some "Shavetail" Lieutenant. That did it. He called the MP's.

One of the doctors passing by caught part of the conversation, and when he heard the name, "Christian," he introduced himself as Stuart's doctor, and called off the MPs. He said Stuart was in pretty bad shape. He had been in a foxhole when a grenade or shell had exploded, and he was sure to lose his badly infected leg, maybe his arm, and possibly his life as well.

He took me in to see a pale, freckle-faced ghost who was out like a light. There was no doubt, it was poor old "Punkey," my Richmond neighbour, looking as though he was breathing his last. I was quite shaken.

These were the days when sulphanilamide was the miracle drug, but it didn't seem to be working. The doctor said there was a new one they had on hand but hadn't tried, called 'penicillin'. They could take off his leg now and possibly save his life or try this new drug. If it killed the infection, there was hope, but if it didn't, they would more than likely lose him.

There wasn't time to contact his family, and to my horror, the doctor was looking to me. I told him as I had known Christian, he wouldn't want to be crippled, and if there was any chance, even at the risk of his life, he would go for the penicillin. Yet, the final decision rested with him, the doctor. I told him I would check back in a few days, but if things looked bad, he was to call me at Lulsgate.

The CO's Magister.

The CO was good enough to delay my posting back to Hawarden and six days later I returned to Upavon prepared for the worst. There was no transport to be had, and it was a long walk to the hospital, but this time I had no trouble with the damned Adjutant and was led straight back to Stuart's room. Trying not to cause any disturbance, I opened the door quietly. What a sight! He was sitting up in bed feeding a nurse chocolates and looking as hale and hearty as I had ever seen him. The doctor came in, looking very pleased with himself, told me the stuff had worked better than he had hoped and that "Punkey" should be on the way home in no time. What a relief for all three of us!

The four-mile walk back to Upavon should have been enjoyable; it was a warm early fall afternoon with not a cloud in the sky. It was an endless landscape, and as described, "not a tree or bush in sight." The only traffic was an occasional cyclist. Halfway to the aerodrome, a typical English cloudburst appeared out of nowhere. It started to rain, and I mean it really poured. Not having a mackintosh, dressed in my best blues and with no place to hide, I was soon a soaking mess. The flight back was cold and wet, but it hardly dampened my relief about Sergeant Christian's miraculous recovery.

39. Hawarden Again

I was put in charge of A Flight and given the task of converting the other instructors to the Harvard. It was a simple machine to fly and a delight when practicing low-level reconnaissance or aerobatics.

Because there hadn't been much point in going on leave and wandering alone around London or Chester, I was more than happy to stay and fly so the others could take a few days off to visit their families. I enjoyed the flying, and there was always a friendly group around the bar at the end of the day – people one knew and who shared the same experiences in everyday life. I was never lonesome and very pleased to have been selected as Officer in Charge of A Flight.

I had never met Wing Commander Parkerhurst, our Engineering Officer, but they asked that I check him out in a Harvard. We met at A Flight's dispersal the next morning, and I was more than mildly surprised to see an officer of at least fifty-five or sixty years of age, six feet tall, thin, and completely bald. He introduced himself, and after a few pleasantries, we had the erks fix him up with a "brolly," (parachute) a helmet and goggles, and off we went.

We flew around a bit before we tried a landing. He was a little rough on the first and second attempts, and I could tell he was a bit discouraged. On the next go, I applied just enough pressure on the control column to ease us to an acceptable landing without his realizing what I had done.

He looked at me, and his face was one of complete joy. Now that he thought he had the hang of it, he didn't want to quit. We repeated the performance and he, still unaware of my subtle assistance, made several excellent landings. Back on the ground he let it be known to all present that "Smithy is the greatest instructor in all of No. 41 OTU. He had me making perfect landings after the second try and I haven't flown an aircraft since 1916 when I was in the Royal Flying Corps!"

As he was leaving and in front of all the others, he invited me for supper in his private quarters the next evening, saluted me (!) and walked off with the cocky step of a twenty-one-year old. The supper was delightful and he quickly dispelled his reputation of being a disagreeable old fogy. He told me of having lost one son the previous year and another was still in North Africa, and hadn't been heard from in six months, enough to sour anyone. I didn't stay long but when I left, I knew I had made a friend.

40. The Piccadilly Commandos

"All work and no play..." you know the rest. The Wing Commander in charge of flying, Eric Plumtree, decided we were working too hard and sent us, two at a time, to London on 48-hour leave. My "cobber" was Flight Lieutenant Robin Jones, a quiet chap who usually kept to himself and when not flying could be found reading or working the *Times* crossword puzzle. But appearances can be deceptive…

It was a long train ride and we spent most of it nipping on a bottle of Scotch. With each sip he became more and more loquacious and was quite amusing, telling of his younger days and describing some of his schoolboy pranks. By the time we reached London, it was dusk. We both had a good 'buzz' on but were still managing to retain the air of sobriety and dignity befitting officers. When registering for a room in the Piccadilly Hotel, Robin was most insistent that it be a double, in front of the hotel on Piccadilly, and he wouldn't take "no" for an answer. I assumed he wanted a front room because of the possible view of an air raid or a buzz bomb. Boy, was I wrong!

The night manager showed us to our room, in front, as requested, with a large window facing the street; he gave Jones the room key, wished us goodnight and retreated. Jones immediately flipped off the lights, drew back the blackout curtains, raised the window and, as I watched horrified, reared back and threw the key out as far as he could. I thought he had lost his mind – too much flying, or something like that.

He noticed the look on my face and broke out laughing.

"Don't panic, Smithy! It's an old trick we used to use when visiting on a free weekend from school. We called it 'room key trolling'. Just wait and watch."

I had heard about the many "ladies of the evening" – known as "Piccadilly Commandos" – who paraded the crowded, dark sidewalks at night. When competition was increased by the arrival of "enthusiastic amateurs" into the market, they were there in daytime as well. They became so bold, that on a subsequent visit to town, I was solicited even though I was walking arm in arm with a pretty young WAAF.

I could hardly believe it, but I was beginning to get the idea, and, sure enough, in about five minutes there was a knock on the door. He opened it and there they stood, two young "ladies", smiling, nicely dressed, one twirling the room key. Feigning innocence, Jones invited them in, trying to explain how he had inadvertently dropped the key while opening the window. It was all so obvious that we broke out laughing, and after a sip or two, they invited us to dinner at a very fancy restaurant – on us, of course. It turned out to be a lovely dinner, but expensive, due to their capacity for champagne.

Jones introduced me to another piece of interesting hotel procedure adopted by those in and around London. It was the custom for male patrons to leave their shoes outside the room door if they wished them to be shined. He cautioned me to be sure they were left with the toes pointing outward. Point them inward toward the door and within the hour, a scantily clad maid would knock, deliver the shoes, and offer any other "services" the occupant may desire. How quaint!

Back at the station a few days later, the same old "Jonesy" was back in his corner, quietly working on his crossword puzzle. Still waters run deep…

Most of my flying was day-instruction in aerobatics, low-level reconnaissance, formation, etc, which was enjoyable, as I have said, except for the occasions when a language barrier arose. The French and Polish students were not familiar with English. Their vocabulary was limited to "yes sir," "no sir," "okay," and "ay haz to use ze pizzer." In the daytime we could see whether they really understood, but at night it was a different story. Night flying with them was a horror. Because of my familiarity with the Harvard, my name appeared as night duty instructor with great regularity.

Off we would go, roaring down a dimly lit flarepath that faded into nothing as we disappeared into the blackness at the end of the runway, the instructor handling the controls in the rear cockpit and the student following his movements up front. Once clear of the aerodrome, flying on instruments, the instructor would demonstrate a gentle left turn and then ask, "Do you understand?" The reply was invariably, "Yesss Sir." The instructor would then say, "Okay, you have it," and the aircraft would continue on its course with no left turn. The instructor would try once again, "You have it, land the bloody thing!" "Yesss Sir," again the response.

Back on the ground, the student, having not even moved the controls, would be all grins as the irate instructor berated, "You bloody fool, don't you understand English?!" "Yesss Sir" would come the answer. It was hopeless, but it went on night after night, until it was finally agreed to restrict their night flying until a French or Polish speaking instructor could be found.

A bright spot was the snow we had at Christmas. On the night of our Christmas party, I stepped outside the mess with a drink in hand and gazed down on the silent, snow-covered hangars and runways. Under the nearly full moon, the scene was truly beautiful. Strangely, I felt a sadness when I realized that the day would soon come when the war would be over, and if I survived, I'd be sent home. I missed Mother and Father and would love to see them again, but I hated the thought of leaving the RAF.

Meanwhile, the party had become a serious celebration. It had seemed as though I had been outside for only a few minutes, but it must have been longer. Everyone was smashed, and I had a lot to do to catch up. I must have succeeded because I didn't remember seeing the station's most beautiful WAAF and my friend "Jonesy" playing "dog and master" in the nude, she leading him around by a red Christmas ribbon tied to his "you-know-what" as a leash.

The CO walked in on the performance and they were posted the next afternoon. Just what they wanted, a Boxing Day present. They, as did many others, despised the little "SOB."

41. Another Sad Loss

Billy Hill, a friend from Richmond, got my telephone number from Mrs Dexter and called me to say he was stationed at Norwich on a B-24 Squadron led by my old friend, Carl Fleming, the brother of John, one of my fellow students at CAA school. What a nice surprise; I had no idea either one was in England. As I was still in charge of A Flight, and had access to a Hurricane any time there was one available, I agreed that I would fly over to Norwich for lunch the next afternoon.

After the austere meals I had become used to, our "lunch" was like a Thanksgiving dinner. We had been eating and talking for the better part of an hour when Billy suggested we pay a call on Carl. According to Billy, Carl had completed his tour, and had been replaced as CO the day before. He should have been in his quarters preparing to go home.

We were met by his orderly, who told us that Colonel Fleming had gone on a raid that morning as an observer and wasn't expected back until late evening. I had to return to base, so after bidding Billy good-bye, I left at dusk. When I landed, there was a message to call Billy. Carl hadn't returned; they had been shot down.

Just recently, a mutual friend told me he had been on the ground watching B-24's dropping supplies to troops along a river in Germany and at that time, the same day that Carl was lost, he saw two 24's shot down. One of them had to have been Carl. That was the mission he had been on.

42. No Help from 'Darkie'

As we were part and parcel of Training Command our instructors were frequently called on to visit other OTUs to demonstrate any expertise we might have that they were lacking.

A photographic unit at Ouston – an OTU up north on the outskirts of Newcastle-on-Tyne – had had a problem taking vertical overlaps as well as oblique photographs with their cameras and was calling for help. The technique was really rather uncomplicated provided the photographic department did their job properly. The cameras were internally mounted and controlled by the pilot but set for altitude and speed by the ground crew. All the pilot had to do was fly at the proper altitude at the predetermined speed (these parameters could be adjusted by the pilot while in flight) and push the control button. A mark on the trailing edge of the mainplane was sighted on the target while the aircraft was flown straight and level for an oblique overlap, and the nose of the aircraft was used as a sight for vertical overlaps. However, flying straight and level over enemy territory made one an ideal target for their antiaircraft gunners.

My experience with photography while on 225 Squadron was in my records and I assume that's why I was summoned to the Chief Flying Instructor's office one miserable, dripping morning. It had been raining for two days and while the weather wizards were predicting improvement by noon there was little or no sign of any let up except for a few ragged tears in the almost solid, eight hundred foot overcast. Typical weather for that time of year in Cheshire, so near the Welsh hills. Three days of fog and falling weather, a moment or two of sunshine, then back to its old stuff, was the norm.

The Chief Flying Instructor was Wing Commander Eric Plumtree, a delightful chap and one of the most popular senior officers on the staff. Five foot four with his shoes on, towheaded and with blue eyes, he resembled a miniature Viking.

"Smithy," he said, "there is a clapped-out Hurricane down at Flights that's equipped with vertical and oblique cameras. Now if you can get that old sod up to Newcastle I think you might be able to help them get their act together."

I looked out of his window at the now pouring rain and he followed my gaze as well as my thoughts and said, "This stuff is reported to improve shortly and the overcast tops are at five thousand. The forecast is for clearing up north so you shouldn't have any trouble. You know this is not an order ... you decide."

There really wasn't much I could do other than "volunteer." Besides, I thought it might be nice to get away for a while.

They trundled the old battle-scarred Hurricane out to a concrete hardstand and I went through the pre-flight check. Not a case of "nothing dripping, nothing hanging, let's go" this time, but instead a thorough going-over with the engine fitters, airframe riggers and instrument and wireless bashers. All seemed to be in order. The fuel and oil were topped off and I was ready to go. A final check with the Met office showed little change except the winds aloft up to 5,000 feet had increased to 20 mph from the NW and were veering to the NE. Cloud and visibility remained the same.

My plan was to climb through the overcast to five thousand and proceed on top in the hope that things would improve by the time I reached Newcastle. Little did I know...

I taxied out, ran up the engine, checked the mags, lined up on the runway, set the altimeter to the field height and the directional gyro to the proper heading… and pushed the throttle wide open. After takeoff, I selected wheels "up" and, being careful to stay below the overcast while turning onto the course to Ouston, began my climb up through the mess.

Once I was in it, it was solid and dark, like grey cotton. It felt like I could reach out and grab a handful. It took a while before I broke out on top at 5,000 feet and what a treat it was – a beautiful snow-white layer of fluff stretching as far as the eye could see, and above, an endless ceiling of blue. Hard to believe soggy old Blighty was less than a mile below.

The climb had taken about ten minutes (although it seemed at least an hour) and now that I was level and the speed had picked up to 140 mph I should be there in approximately 60 minutes.

I checked the gages - fuel, oil pressure, etc, and all were reading properly, so I eased my bottom into a more comfortable position on the ever-present life raft package sandwiched between me and the parachute pack and sat back to enjoy the flight…

The enjoyment turned to worry a short time later when I realized the weather hadn't begun to improve and I was still above the overcast with no definite idea where I was except by "dead reckoning" (I always hated that term).

Back during our training days the Flight Sergeant in charge of the navigation course told us on many occasions that we must be aware that the forever-changing weather in England could result in being unsure of one's location when in or above an overcast. He would then add "Do not forget 'DARKIE' and do not hesitate to use it. It is always on VHF channel 'C' (I'm not absolutely sure of the channel, but I seem to recall it was 'C'). DARKIE was a radar system made up of a number of stations throughout England that tracked aircraft that were sending out a signal on their IFF (Identifacation Friend or Foe). I had never tried it, but this would be a good time to see what they could do.

"Hello DARKIE, hello DARKIE…"

No response. Try again.

"Hello DARKIE, hello DARKIE…"

Still no response. The buggers must be asleep. But after many more attempts I reached the conclusion that either my calls were not getting out or they were too busy to answer them.

I thought it wasn't a very good idea to keep pressing on not having any idea of my location so I started slowly circling and descending into the overcast top, hoping there just might be a break in the murk.

I was lucky – half way round my second orbit, there it was … a slight thinning and what appeared to be the ground. I eased the control column forward to increase my rate of decent and as I did it became clearer and we were soon scooting along beneath the cloud. Still with no idea where I was, I kept widening my orbit, straining to see something to identify. I noticed with astonishment that I was in a valley, surrounded on all sides by hills and directly below me was an airdrome!

I performed the fastest circuit and landing I had ever made, taxied over to the control tower and climbed out, trying to disguise my perspiration from the erk chocking the wheels. A Flight Lieutenant with a couple of ribbons on his tunic, flying a Hurricane certainly can't – or won't – admit he is lost. The conversation that took place while we were refuelling must have been a classic. I tried every way I could to find out the name of the station without asking and giving the game away, but I think he must have known. After he finished he helped me buckle my harness, wished me luck, slipped off the wing and with a wide knowing smile, saluted as I started up.

As I taxied out I called the tower requesting a heading to Ouston and the weather. Same old thing, clearing about twenty miles ahead, but the surface winds at Ouston were now reported to be SIXTY mph out of the north. That was going to make it difficult to hold the thing on the ground once we landed.

Sure enough, upon arrival I found it as advertised and the control tower issued a warning, suggesting I seek an alternative airdrome. But they didn't say where.

I refused their suggestion and requested permission to land. They acknowledged in the affirmative and offered a crew of erks to help when I touched down. Once I was in the circuit, when heading upwind I appeared to be crawling, but when headed downwind it was a different story. Never have I seen a Hurricane move so quickly. Turning on the approach, again I slowed to a crawl. The ground crew was there as I touched down. It was impossible to perform the usual stalled landing – every time I lowered the tail the darn thing wanted to leap in the air again. I held it on its main undercarriage and with the help of two erks on each wing we managed to taxi at almost full throttle into the lee of a hangar. They tied it down there, not daring to open the hangar doors against the wind.

No photos that day, but when it became more peaceful on the morrow we accomplished what we had set out to do.

I am sure I finally found out the name of that station, but failed to enter it in my logbook, so it remains unknown. As for DARKIE – I questioned a number of my fellow pilots and never found anyone who had used it successfully.

43. A Brush with the CO

The weather became a real problem. There was snow on the ground most of the time, and when the temperature rose only a few degrees, the entire area was locked in a dense fog. When it lifted to a few hundred feet and the visibility improved to a half mile or more, the Flight Commanders were called on, in turn, to do a "weather reccy."

I hated it. It entailed a climb up through the stuff to determine its thickness. Having no idea of the height of the top, one could only climb to a predetermined altitude, and if there was no break, start back down, hoping it hadn't closed in completely since takeoff. In order to maintain a general idea where I was, I would climb and descend in a constant rate of turn. This method worked, but it was still exciting when the altimeter showed only six or eight hundred feet, and you were still in cloud and not entirely sure where the hills were.

My six months' duty as an instructor (in lieu of rest) was coming to completion in a few weeks, when I dropped a major "clanger." Returning from low-level formation practice with a student, we entered the circuit at Hawarden on the downwind leg, and I did a slow roll, a prerogative usually allowed instructors. I had hardly touched down when ground control announced over the Tannoy for all the station to hear, "The pilot of Hurricane 354, Flight Lieutenant Smith, is to report to HQ immediately." I didn't know what to expect, but I was sure it would be of great interest. I also didn't know that they had posted in Daily Routine Orders the day before, "Aerobatics are prohibited within a radius of three miles of the aerodrome."

These orders were supposed to be read by everyone every day, but I missed this one – a cardinal sin.

Dressed as required and on the way to HQ, I was stopped by Wing Commander Plumtree. He knew the problem was the slow roll and suggested that I deny it. Although the Group Captain had seen the manoeuvre, he would be unable to prove I was the pilot. There had been five or six Hurricanes in the circuit at the time. But I disliked the little wretch so much that I hated for him to have me in a position to tell a lie. After all, the worst he could do was "fire" me, and anyway, I was so close to completing my term that I would be leaving shortly.

I was ushered into his office by his nice WAAF Adjutant, who by all reports was terrified of him. As she was closing the door, she whispered encouragement, "Keep your pecker up." (Be brave.) I saluted and stood there about two minutes, a seeming eternity, before he glared up at me, his little moustache twitching, and demanded, "Was that you rolling the Hurricane in the circuit."

I answered, "Yes, Sir."

"Why?" he asked.

"I guess it was sheer exuberance, Sir."

Then here it came; "Have you read Daily Routine Orders?"

"No, Sir," I said. That seemed to enrage him.

"Don't you realize that's the same as doing this to me?" he asked, thumbing his nose.

"That wasn't my intent, Sir."

"Be that as it may, this is what I'm going to do with your application to attend Aircraft Fighter Development School in Texas." With that, he tore the papers into shreds and threw them into a nearby waste basket. I really didn't care. There wasn't much hope that I would be accepted, and since applying I had pretty much decided to stay in England until the war was over.

"Furthermore," he went on, "I am going to see that you are immediately posted to one of the last operational Squadrons in the UK, No. 65 in Peterhead, Scotland. You are to be packed and ready to go in 48 hours. That is all."

I could hardly keep from laughing. The AOC at Adastral House in London hadn't forgotten me. He was as good as his word; No. 65 was flying Mustangs! The bloody little sod didn't know what I knew and wanted me to believe that sending me on Ops was his idea of a proper punishment. I saluted and left him wondering why I was smiling.

No 65 Squadron was located on the north-east coast of Scotland as shown on the map below.

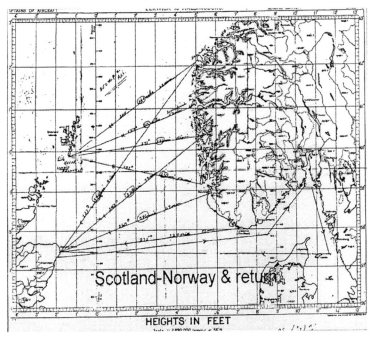

44. 65 Squadron, Peterhead

I was flown up to Peterhead, the northernmost point on the East Coast of Scotland, on the edge of the North Sea. They didn't waste any time. I was introduced to Flight Lieutenant Williams, CO of B Flight and Squadron Leader Ian Stewart, Squadron Commander, who had been at Hawarden when I was there in 1942. The next day was spent flying locally, getting familiar with the tits and tabs on the new Mustang Mark III. It was very much like its predecessors except for the throttle lever, the new gyro-controlled gun sight, and the sliding cockpit canopy. In order to carry enough fuel for 1000 to 1500 mile trips, they had added a 60-gallon tank behind the pilot and two 100-gallon external papier-mâché wing tanks. They looked like big bombs.

Upon reaching 1500 feet after takeoff, we were to switch to these "tip tanks" to make sure they were feeding properly. If they failed the test, we were supposed to return, and land, still full of fuel. I thought it was rather stupid to endanger a pilot and aircraft that way just to save 200 gallons of fuel and two paper tanks. Normal approach speed was 130 mph, but because of the additional weight, I used an airspeed of 145 on one occasion and as I flared out, about three feet above the runway, the thing stalled and dropped a wing. Had I been a couple of feet higher not only I, but the Aerodrome Control Pilot at the entrance of the runway, and possibly a few other aircraft would have become one big fireball. I mentioned this incident to the Flight Commander and the response was, "These things are rather unpredictable with all that extra weight."

We had a session of night takeoffs and landings without mishap. The Mustang was not designed to be a night fighter but we were frequently required to leave in the dark in order to be over the targets at sunup. Our assignments entailed flying protective cover for the rocket-firing Beaufighters and Mosquitos on anti-shipping strikes up in the fjords and coastal harbours of Norway. They would leave before us, and we being faster, would pick them up at sea level off the Scottish coast.

From our officers' billets to the dispersal area, we had about a two-mile walk along a narrow, unpaved, dusty lane lined with small farm houses. Half-asleep as we walked in the early morning darkness, we would hear voices. Hands would reach across the fence offering a couple of precious eggs for our breakfast with a heartfelt "God bless ye, lads." What wonderful people. They were there every morning before sunrise, fair weather or foul.

I had thought it strange that so many pilots; Ian Stewart, Robert Weighill, and James Young to name a few, were drawn from Hawarden. As I have mentioned, Hawarden was an Army Cooperation Training Unit that specialized in low-level work and not fighter training. My first operational flight revealed the answer. In order to stay below the enemy's radar, all aircraft were required to fly no higher than twenty feet above the wave tops and lower whenever possible. Absolute radio silence had to be observed. All signals were given by hand or waggling of wings.

On a windy day when the seas were running high, salt water spray became a problem. I was number two to Squadron Leader Johnny Foster on my first trip. It was a particularly windy day, and a freak wave broke high enough for mist from the salt spray to cover his windscreen. After an hour, barely able to see and unable to find a rain storm to clear the salt, he decided we should abort. This was the only time I was unable to complete a sortie.

ABERDEEN BON-ACCORD AND NORTHERN PICTORIAL. —Thursday, April 26, 1945

SORRY—YOU'RE DEPRIVED
OF THE PLEASURE OF
DANCING AT
ABERDEEN'S LEADING BALLROOM
FOR DISCRIMINATING DANCERS
1945

Palais-de-Danse

MEANTIME CLOSED FOR
THE ANNUAL VACATION.

Re-opens Friday, 11th May
I — Worth Waiting For — !

Aberdeen Bon-Accord
and Northern Pictori

w Series No. 1012.   [REGISTERED AT THE GENERAL POST OFFICE AS A NEWSPAPER]   THURSDAY, APRIL 26, 1945.   Born 1880.

Must:

ONE of the Mustangs takes off on a trial spin before the serious work begins. Based in Scotland, these fighters are providing fighter cover for Coastal Command rocket-firing Mosquitoes which are harrying enemy shipping off the Norwegian coast

RIGHT — Flying Officer Maynard tests his controls.

MEET THE BOYS

ABOVE—Squadron Leader John Foster, D.F.C. (seated in tre), who has had notable ... in leading attacks on the my. With him are members his squadron, who, since Jan... have destroyed fourteen ... and scored eight "prob-..."

ELOW—Squadron Leader Peter Hearne, who has shot down ... enemy fighters off Norway. ... third from left, back row. ... members of his squadron.

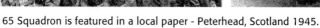

65 Squadron is featured in a local paper - Peterhead, Scotland 1945.

Sadly, my friend, and a Squadron Leader, Ian Graham Stewart, was lost on that same day. The next day, Squadron Leader Hill was killed over Lister, Norway.

Three days later, we were to escort forty-five Beaufighters on a shipping strike in the harbour of Aalsund, Norway. Again, it was a takeoff in the blackness at 4:00 am. One had to fumble around with the aid of a shielded torch held by one of the erks, seeking 'chute snaps and buckles and harness straps. There was enough light from the gentle glow of the red cockpit light to locate the switches and instruments, but outside, it was as dark as the inside of a derby hat.

Foster, my number one, was faintly visible in his cockpit forty feet away, and as soon as all was ready, he signalled "start up." The engine was primed with two or three shots from the Kygas primer, "clear" was shouted to the erk standing by the battery cart, ignition switches were turned on, and at a thumbs-up signal, we pressed the energizer button. The propeller turned two or three times, and the engine burst into life with a roar and a blinding burst of blue flame and smoke.

Throttled back to a gentle idle, things quieted down a bit, and the flaming glare from the exhaust stacks subsided enough for the tiny pinpoints of Foster's riding lights to be seen. We snaked out, in order to see ahead of that long nose, as we followed the little hooded lights along the taxi path to the main runway. I lined up as close as possible, my wing tip only a few feet from his, and waited for the green flash from the hooded Aldis lamp at the control tower. Foster, as the leader, acknowledged the signal by flicking his lights, indicating we were on our way. Throttles were slowly opened to maximum power, and as soon as we were airborne, not daring to take my eyes off him for a second, I reached down, found the undercart lever, selected wheels up and got those little green lights indicating they were up and locked.

The Lads of #65 - Smithy, kneeling 2nd from right.

Streaks of light on the horizon heralded the arrival of dawn, and it became easier to keep station as we circled, waiting for the rest to join up. There were twelve of us with one extra in attendance to take the place of anyone who might have a malfunction on the way out.

Behind in the distance, we could see the swarm of Beaufighters racing to catch up. As the light improved, the deadly-looking rockets under their wings were clearly visible. We slowed a bit until they were abreast of us and then we all dove to just above wave height as we crossed the Scottish coast. We switched to the auxiliary wing tanks, spread the formation out and settled down for what would become a four-hour, thirty-minute sortie.

Aalsund was three hundred miles south of the Arctic Circle and one hundred miles south of Tromso, where the German battleship, "Tirpitz," had been hiding. The Beaus were to search for and destroy any enemy shipping or transport in or around the harbour and, we were to remain two to three thousand feet above as protection.

For miles around, all that could be seen, was a wave of aircraft undulating up and down trying to maintain a loose formation at the same low level. Kept busy monitoring instruments and judging altitude, I failed to see the Norwegian coast until we were almost upon it. Never having been in this part of the world, I was fascinated by the beauty and ruggedness of the snow-covered cliffs. Even at this distance, the entrances to several fjords were quite obvious. At a given signal, our Squadron climbed up, switched on guns and gun sights, and then released the auxiliary wing tanks, each making sure to be slightly above those ahead to avoid being clobbered as they fell.

The Beaus headed for the harbour, and we broke up into sections of two to patrol the coastline while they searched for shipping. There was little or no ground fire, so Foster led us down into a fjord to look for any type of military installation or hidden shipping. The fjords were so narrow and steep that it was impossible to climb out at the inshore end, so the best approach was to enter from the inshore end. Down on the water's surface, closed in by those towering stone cliffs, twisting and turning at 300 mph or more, was exhilarating to say the least!

Just as we reached the opening to the sea, the shore batteries on the cliff tops opened up. It was a great surprise to find ourselves flying through a curtain of machine gun fire with tracers coming down at us instead of up. We were lucky to escape and remembered to mark our charts that this was an area to be avoided.

Meanwhile, the Beaufighters had damaged three ships. No enemy aircraft were reported, so we all headed for home at the prearranged hour. Radar being of no concern, we could choose any altitude we liked, but the two-hour trip back was still very uncomfortable. We were relaxed but tired, and with the sun glaring in our eyes and the soothing drone of the Merlin, it was difficult to stay awake. Several times, I found it necessary to pinch or slap myself to keep from nodding off.

Beaufighter rockets headed for shipping - Borgestad, Norway Mar 30 1945.

On a sortie two days later, we spent the better part of an hour searching the Norwegian coast for Flight Lieutenant Watt, who was last seen by one of his mates over the sea in an inverted position, trailing smoke. Sadly, we found no trace of his aircraft or his dinghy.

We attacked the east Coast of Norway on several occasions, and most of those strikes took place in the early morning in order to have the sun behind us as we arrived. We had been up near Oslo, where the Mosquitos had a successful raid, and we were returning home along the coast at about 500 feet above the "Mossies," who were flying at tree top level. Two Squadrons of twelve aircraft, ours, No. 65, and our sister Squadron, No. 19, were all flying wing tip to wing tip, No. 19 a little ahead and slightly below. Why, I never knew. We were all so occupied with trying to keep station and not run into each other that it was hard to take a look around – another cardinal sin!

But I was new on the Squadron, and since the Squadron Leaders were old hands, I felt they knew what they were doing. Still, I was worried, and I wondered how we were allowed to tear up all these places with no opposition. While we did have air superiority, the enemy hadn't, as yet, quit. I had spent a lot of time on 225 Squadron as a number two, weaving and checking on what might be behind, and out of habit, I chanced to glance up and over my right shoulder, looked again and froze.

Twelve FW 190s were at 4 o'clock about 5000 feet above. They were trailing white vapour from their water injection systems, which made them quite easy to identify, and they were coming like bats-out-of-hell. I waited a moment, thinking that someone else out of our whole gaggle must see them, but the R/T was silent. I pushed the transmit button and called: "Red Leader, a dozen bandits at 4 o'clock and high." The response was, "Okay, red section close up."

What?! Why didn't some of us turn into them? Maybe he didn't understand me. I called again, "Red Leader, there are twelve 190s at 4 o'clock at 5000 feet above," and got the same reply, "Close up." There was nothing left for me to do but follow instructions.

I held my breath and scrunched down behind the armour-plated seat waiting for the crash of cannon shells and machine gun bullets. In less than a minute, it happened. A Mosquito below and right in front of me burst into flames and crashed into a hillside as two 190s streaked up almost vertically through the Squadron formation.

I was astonished! We kept grinding along for a good ten precious seconds as though nothing had happened." What the hell is the matter with these people?" I thought. Then the Squadron Leader called out, "Smithy, you and your number two, go after them." That was us, Warrant Officer Abbott and me. No response was necessary. I could still see the two 190s as we broke hard left, but I had no idea where the other ten were. I had a strange feeling when I glanced back at our Squadrons disappearing in the distance.

Maximum power got us within range very quickly, but they saw us, and realizing we were catching up, started a steep left-hand circle. The aircraft were pretty evenly matched, so round and round we went, me behind a 190, a 190 behind me, and Abbott behind him. No one seemed to be gaining any advantage. I realized then that Mustangs were great for strafing at this altitude but they were more in their element higher up, not dog fighting down where we were. They couldn't come close to matching the nimbleness or turning radius of a Spit at this level. (I will probably hear considerable argument on this point.)

Cannon shell tracers from the 190 behind me were streaming by just below and about twenty feet from my wing tip while I was trying to get a bead on the one in front as he was firing at Abbott. This continued for at least five minutes, and at full power. I guessed we were burning almost two gallons of fuel a minute. Fuel wasn't the only problem. The other 190s were around somewhere and could bounce us at any time. These two had to be aware of our fuel situation and knew if they kept us at bay long enough, we would have had it.

I called Abbott and said, "The next time around, you break off. I'll cover you for one more turn and then follow." He did as suggested, I followed him in turn, and we both headed down to sea level, flat out, throttles "through the gate." This low, we could outrun anything they had, and we did. But we had no idea what lay ahead for the hundred miles to, and around the southern tip of Norway, where we should make a turn to the west towards our base in Scotland.

The Luftwaffe had a very active group at Stavanger on the southwest coast, which was manned by several Squadrons of ME 109s and FW 190s. It was usually avoided when returning low on petrol from these strikes. The drill was to fly at least twenty miles south beyond the coastline before making the turn to the west, but under the circumstances, I felt we should use the shortest route available and take our chances.

We were as low as we could get as we crossed the coast a few miles south of Stavanger. We could see the aerodrome had no signs of activity, so we throttled back to extend our range, and climbed to two thousand feet. I heaved a sigh of relief, cracked the canopy open for fresh air, and fumbled for the piece of chocolate I usually carried in the pocket of my Mae West. Abbott came up alongside, flying loose formation and gave a thumbs-up.

Relief from the mental anxiety and physical effort of the last hour plus the warmth of the cockpit and drone of the Merlin brought back a pleasant state of euphoria, so I loosened my Sutton harness and the uncomfortable oxygen mask containing the VHF microphone. While I was puzzling over the Squadron Leader's order to "close up" in response to my report of bandits, I happened to glance over at Abbott, and my eye caught movement astern.

There were four aircraft a half-mile away and 500 feet below, closing fast. "Whizzo," I thought, believing that part of the Squadron had come looking for us, "How thoughtful." For a moment, I almost felt a surge of "esprit de corps" but then I looked again... They were coming full-tilt, not Mustangs, but 109s, hoping to catch us unaware, and here I was with loosened harness and loose face mask containing my VHF mike. With the control column between my knees, I played the fastest two-handed game ever, as I attempted to get rid of the chocolate, tighten my harness and hook up the mask all at the same time.

Finally, I called Abbott and told him we had bandits under our rear, but to carry on until I made a move. We were only a few feet apart, and I could see him nod his head in understanding.

I waited for them to come within firing range, and as soon as they raised their noses to fire, I called, "Break left," and we rolled into a steep 180, heading directly at them. We obviously caught them by surprise. The bastards thought they had a sure thing. They scattered. There were aircraft everywhere, each trying to get a shot at the other. I had no idea where it came from, but one passed in front of me in a vertical dive so close I could almost make out the fasteners on his cowling. He was so quick it was useless to fire. We twisted and turned and dove and climbed trying to resist the forces of gravity and not black out, at the same time looking ahead and behind for the 109s. I had the idea; I'll pull straight up and see if the one behind slides underneath. I tried it, rolled over at the top, looked down as he did as expected and then they were gone. Except for us, the sky was empty. I found it hard to believe they could disappear so quickly. Taking another careful look around, we dropped down to sea level, and once more, headed for home.

Once I was sure we were clear, and again feeling Churchill's "exhilaration," I removed my mask and settled back to relax for the last few moments before we reached Peterhead. I knew a gross error had been made at the expense of two lads and a wonderful aircraft, but what to do or say about it? For the first time, I was unable to feel the relief that usually came when returning to base unscathed.

We arrived after the others and were late for debriefing. When asked, we explained our "adventures" to the Intelligence Officer without too much detail. The CO had only one comment: "Smithy, when you report enemy aircraft in the future, remember to identify yourself." This instead of, "Good show for reporting those bandits." I was a bit ticked off. No, I was *really pissed!* Red Leader had known it was me all the while.

I have often wondered about his unexplained comment, and why he didn't order us to attack as soon as the 190s were reported instead of waiting until we lost the Mosquito. I also wonder why I, with so little experience on this Squadron, was placed in charge of a section. In any event, I was glad to have Warrant Officer Abbott as my number two. The only drawback was that he was a non-commissioned officer and under British regulations he was not allowed to use the officers' mess; a stupid rule. Consequently, the only time we saw each other was at Flights. He was a decent chap and a good pilot and should have had a commission.

By March of 1945 the news on the BBC was good. We were winning! However, many more lives would be lost before there would be total and complete victory. We still had to get on with it. As the last Operational Squadron stationed in England, we began our own private little war. Our assignments continued to be strikes against enemy shipping and their protective submarine escorts in an attempt to strangle their ability to move their ships, ammunition and troops.

Early one morning we set out to escort twenty-four Mossies for a strike in a harbour just south of Oslo. In order to confuse the enemy, our route took us across Denmark and over the Kattegat sea. Here we would turn north and follow the Skagerrak up toward Oslo, everyone staying at zero feet.

When we crossed the western coast of Denmark, there occurred the most heart-warming display of support I had ever witnessed. The terrain was mostly farmland and flat as a pancake. As we swept across the grain fields, we were so low that at times we flew beneath power lines. I could see paths in the grain being flattened by the prop-wash of the aircraft alongside. Occasionally we had to lift up over horse-drawn hay wagons and the farmers working in the fields. As we passed overhead, I could see their upturned faces as they threw their hats in the air, shouting and waving us on. Very moving.

The raid was a success. They sank three ships just off Denmark but we lost Flight Lieutenant Bradford; no one seemed to know what had happened to him.

Flight Lieutenant Graham Pearson had a forced landing in Sweden when his engine packed up and when we returned I was sent down in the Squadron's Proctor to pick him up at Aberdeen. The Swedish underground had kindly flown him over, but I almost killed us both trying to land back at Peterhead in a sudden, unpredicted snowstorm.

We arrived over the field on top of the junk, low on fuel. I looked at Graham and he looked at me, shrugged as if to say, "Ah, so be it," then we both saw an opening at the same time. I rolled over and plunged through the hole, almost tearing the little Proctor to pieces, and fortunately, there it was, the runway, partially obscured by rain and snowflakes. How could conditions change so quickly, I wondered? But then, I knew very little about Scottish weather. Their "auld" saying was, "If you don't like it now, just wait a few minutes; it'll change."

Pearson and I were in the same hut and became quite good friends in the short time we were together. We used to do a bit of pub crawling on the outskirts of Peterhead and one of his favourites was the "Pussycats and The Fiddle" – Well named, the place was usually jammed full of thirsty cats of the two legged variety.

He was quite wealthy, independent of his RAF income, and after he stepped up to the bar and ordered a round of drinks for the house, it wasn't long before he was surrounded by a group of WAAFs as well as Land Army girls, all vying for his attention. He was towheaded, blue eyed and very striking-looking in his dress uniform when we arrived – not a hair out of place – but not for long. In a half hour he became a little loose and after an hour he was a mess, as were most of the "ladies." I would standby in amazement and watch a nice, quiet little pub turn into bedlam with the patrons laughing, singing and shouting at the top of their voices. Spilling beer, wine, whisky and gin all over themselves and anyone nearby. I, as wasted as I was, would have to drag him out and set him off back to our hut in the darkest of night, both of us hanging on to each other to keep from falling off the world.

He kept a pet Ferret in his room called "Ricky Tickki", who would be sleeping peacefully in his cage when we arrived. Pearson would speak to him sweetly and stick his hand in the cage to stroke him. Ricky didn't care to be awakened at that time of night and would slash out with razor sharp teeth, leaving his master's hand bleeding profusely. Never have I heard such language as he used to describe "that ungrateful little sod."

He hadn't wised-up even by the time I left. About once a week he would appear with his hand swathed in a fresh bandage.

45. North Sea Escapades

My WAAF friend, Section Officer Frances Fair, invited me to the first debutante party to be organized in London since the war started. It was to be held at The Ritz and was causing quite a stir. Knowing I didn't sleep well on overnight trains and wanting to arrive 'bright-eyed and bushy-tailed', I asked the MO for a sleeping pill. He gave me two.

Once aboard the train, I stupidly had a few drinks and "opened the hangar doors" with a Flight Sergeant who was sitting across the compartment until I noticed it was after 1:00am. To ensure a good night's sleep, I took both pills and fell into a deep slumber. Upon arrival in London, Frances and the porter had to practically carry me off the train. I really don't remember a thing. However, a few days after my return to Peterhead, I had a letter from her. She told me what a wonderful time I had and how much her friends had admired her escort. He was so quiet and charming, not at all like the Americans they had heard about. He just stood in a corner with a drink in his hand, and smiled.

Of all the RAF stations I had seen, No. 65 was far and away the best. The waitresses and batmen treated us like royalty. The food was better than in Training Command, and although under great stress most everyone, after a few pints of "arf-and-arf," appeared to be quite relaxed and cheerful. There was little enter-tainment except for an occasional evening visit to a pub in Peterhead when we weren't scheduled to fly the next day. We were usually so tired when we returned from our sorties that all we wanted was a short discussion of the day's work, a drink, a good meal, and bed.

Our next effort was escorting thirty Beaufighters, again up to Aalsund Fjord. There had been reports of U-boat activity in the area, prime targets for these rocket-carrying fighter-bombers. It turned into almost a five-hour sweep, and it would have been a total success had not two of the Beau's collided off the Norway coast on the way out.

Both crews ditched successfully and were in the water in their Mae Wests, some in their dinghies. A distress call was made to an Air Sea Rescue (ASR) unit in the Shetlands, and we were told they were on their way. In the meantime, the poor fellows in the water would probably freeze. They could last only fifteen or twenty minutes unless they managed to crawl into one of the dinghies. Even then, those little rafts offered scant protection from the icy waters.

This was all taking place within sight of the Norwegian coast. The Squadron Leader designated six of us (three sections) to stand by to protect them in case there was an attempt by the enemy to interfere. We were circling the area, throttled back as far as possible to save fuel, when the ASR's Wellington arrived carrying a huge lifeboat slung beneath its bomb bay doors. These boats were designed to be dropped via two parachutes fastened fore and aft which automatically released on contact with the sea.

The Wellington circled until it was in position, released the boat and the 'chutes deployed as we all watched with relief. It looked like a perfect drop, well within reach, although slightly downwind of the survivors. All's well that ends well, we thought. But unfortunately, this was not to be. The 'chute on the stern failed to disengage and began towing the boat downwind faster than they could swim or paddle. We dove and fired on it, hoping to tear it loose, but our efforts were in vain. We were low on fuel and were ordered to return to base. It was a tragedy in the making. As we turned to leave, I looked back to see them paddling desperately trying to catch that drifting, life-sustaining haven of comfort and warmth. (We still hadn't learned their fate a month later when I left the Squadron.)

Meanwhile, Abbott and I had a problem of our own. We had stayed a little longer than we should. The others had gone ahead and now fuel was down to a minimum for the long trip home. We throttled back as much as we dared in order to extend our range, and kept our fingers crossed. We were flying about one hundred feet, in air that was crystal clear, but we were just beneath a solid cloud cover. This could mean real trouble when we reached Peterhead, which was situated on top of the cliffs. There, the clouds would be at ground level, enveloping everything in a dense fog. Should a situation such as this occur, and should we not be able to locate an alternate aerodrome, our instructions were to climb-up over land, and if still in cloud, head the aircraft toward the sea, and bail out.

There they were, the cliffs, and as we feared, the clouds were sitting right on top. I called the Controller and was told the visibility was zero-zero and to go to an alternate. That didn't sound good. We had only a few minutes of petrol left and it would take almost that much to climb up high enough to jump. I called Abbott, and suggested we look for Banff, the Mosquito's base, about thirty miles down the coast, situated right at the edge of the cliffs. He agreed, but said if the engine even sputtered, he was going to zoom up into the overcast and bail out. I told him it was to be his choice.

We carried on for a few minutes, sweeping back and forth when we were where we thought Banff should be. We could see nothing but the thick, grey overcast. I was about to suggest that we start our climb to clear out, when through the murk I spotted two sodium lamps that had to mark the end of a runway. I called them to Abbott's attention, and lowering our wheels and sticking close together, we climbed up to the top of the cliff. Using mostly imagination, we landed on the most beautiful, fog-enshrouded runway I had ever seen.

A van appeared out of the mist and led us to a parking spot, and as I was shutting down the engine, Abbott called and said his had just begun to sputter. It quit while we were talking! We had a raucous party with the boys of Banff that night, and flew the kites back to Peterhead the next morning.

The raid had been considered a success. The Mossies had caught a sub on the surface off the Denmark coast, and were credited with its sinking. Again a few days later, we were sent into the Kattegat with the Beaus. They fired on three merchant ships, and sank one with no losses to themselves. We were unopposed in the air, but friend Jim Butler's aircraft was hit by flak on the way out and exploded.

The Mossies get a U-Boat off the coast of Norway.

The end of April '45 arrived, as did my twenty-second and last sortie with No. 65. It was a big one; forty-two Mosquitos, No. 19 Squadron and us. We were to make an antisubmarine strike near the pens where the subs were built. The Mossies attacked three subs as well as a flak ship that had been a problem to the Allied bomber streams. The antiaircraft fire was as thick as I had ever seen. The sky was covered with thick, black bursts from the explosions and as we flew though those that had burst in front, the acrid smell of cordite filled the cockpit.

Three Mosquitos were lost as well as two Mustangs from No. 19. We were lucky, No. 65 lost none and no enemy aircraft were reported.

I remain puzzled by their idea of putting up so many fighters in close formation as protection against marauding enemy aircraft. Close formation requires constant attention to the leader, and a constant speed controlled by continuous throttle adjustments. If they would spread us into a looser formation, everyone would have a better chance to look around, instead of having to concentrate on keeping position and avoiding a collision with the leader's aircraft.

My thoughts frequently go back to those lads in that Mosquito the 190s shot out from under us. Our duty was to protect them and we failed miserably. I know in my heart if we had broken that close formation and turned into those 190s when they were first spotted, there is a good chance those two boys would have survived.

It was not my last sortie by my choice. The CO called me in the next morning and handed me a signal from Air Ministry saying that I was to be posted immediately to Ferry Command. He was as curious as I was. He hadn't requested it and neither had I, and why Ferry Command? Postings usually came from Fighter Command Headquarters, not Air Ministry. This was the beginning of a mystery I have never solved.

46.   I Become a Ferry Pilot

No.12 Ferry Unit was located at Melton Mowbray about 100 miles northwest of London in the middle of nowhere. It was a staging area for different types of mostly single-engine aircraft waiting to be delivered to various destinations overseas. There were quite a few Mustangs standing about and I supposed that they were going to be my job. The pilots were from squadrons all over the country some "tour-expired" and others who, as the Army lads put it, "hadn't seen the elephant" (i.e. they hadn't done any operational flying).

I was scheduled the third day after I arrived. Three others and I were to deliver Mustangs from an airfield near the South Coast, Portreath, to one of my old stamping grounds, Capodicino in Naples. Here, the aircraft were to be picked up by another group for delivery to the Middle East and then on to India and the Far East. Our route was to be via Estre in France and then on to Naples. As our navigational abilities were not trusted, a Mosquito with all the latest radio equipment was assigned to lead us.

We took off under a solid cloud cover at 5,000 feet, joined up in formation and had turned to our proper heading when I noticed the Mossie was continuing to climb. We closed up formation and followed, but when we hit the murk, it became so dense that the Mossie disappeared. I continued to climb, holding a steady compass course and hoped the others would do the same. The Mustang was very good at this, very stable, and less sensitive than most of the other fighters, so stable in fact, that I was almost relaxed... Suddenly there was a blinding flash and a tremendous crash of thunder. I will swear I could see a streak of electricity entering my starboard wing and passing out the port wing. For what seemed to be at least a second, I was a large electrode. The noise and flash of light were frightening, and I fully expected to see pieces flying off, or at the least, fire crawling out of the engine compartment. I remained frozen for a moment, and then checked the gauges. Apart from the compass spinning aimlessly, all appeared to be normal. Had it not been for the ear-splitting noise, I supposed it might have been caused by the aircraft expelling its own static electricity; and possibly that process could be accompanied by thunder. Whatever it was, it gave me one hell of a fright!

One at a time, we popped out at 8,000 feet but the Mosquito was nowhere in sight, only the towering, anvil-shaped cloud of a thunderstorm could be seen far behind. We never saw the Mosquito again. When we landed at Estre, I quizzed the others about the lightning and they had no idea what I had gone through. They just looked at me and shook their heads. There were even mutterings about my being "round the bend." We refuelled and had lunch, and as I was familiar with the Italian coast, they decided to carry on, trusting me to lead them to Naples.

Memories came flooding back as we passed over the mouth of the Tiber, the Pontine Marshes, then Anzio, Nettuno, Gaeta and No 225's landing ground at Lagos. Naples wasn't hard to find; the weather was clear and beautiful and I couldn't resist making a pass over the Sorrentine Peninsula – it is really one of the loveliest spots in the world. We spent the night at Capodicino and returned to Portreath the next afternoon, again in a Wellington.

I had one more trip to Naples a week later, and on my return I found a signal had come through posting me to Transport Command. I had no idea what this was about, and none of the senior officers could help.

47. King's Messenger

Headquarters was at Bushey Park, just outside Richmond in Surrey, and across the park from Hampton Court. (As a note of possible interest; Richmond, Virginia was so named by the then Governor, William Byrd because the view of the James River reminded him of the Thames from Richmond, Surrey.)

I took the train from Portreath up to London, caught one of the locals out to Richmond, and walked along the Thames out to HQ. I reported to the Adjutant, and was told I had been appointed *Mess Secretary*. I was flabbergasted! Of all the duties, flying and otherwise, how on earth could I have been chosen for this one? This was a huge station, with all types of high-ranking brass, not only permanent staff, but also transient personnel on their way to all parts of the world. This required our mess to produce frequent formal dinners for Air Commodores, Air Marshals, two, three and four star US Generals, etc. Fortunately, we had a very efficient staff headed by a very capable WAAF Flight Sergeant, which left me with little to do other than sign papers and approve food purchases. I hated it!

Bushey Park itself was a beautiful English park, like those in London. Filled with deer, swans, ducks and other wildlife, it had several large lakes that had been covered with camouflage netting in order to keep them from being used as landmarks by enemy bombers on moonlit nights. On the side opposite HQ was Hampton Court Palace, as well as one of the most famous, and most expensive, pubs in England, "The Mitre."

Having heard about this place, I thought it might be worth a visit. My WAAF Flight Sergeant and I arrived there about sunset and after a few beers, stepped out into the dark thinking to have a pleasant stroll back to HQ. The park, made up of several hundred acres, was pitch black – not a pinpoint of light anywhere. We started out in what we thought was the right direction but somehow wandered off into the grass and then, without warning, we were wading knee deep in one of the ponds. It was a bit sticky there for a while. We were really lost. As luck would have it, the sky cleared enough for us to be able to make out the North Star, which gave us some sense of direction, but we still couldn't see the lakes until we were in them. It was hours before we found the HQ entrance gates, and we had a lot of explaining to do, as well as a sizable cleaning bill!

On VE Day I had taken a train up to London, and was sitting on the curb of Piccadilly's median strip, alone at midnight, drink in hand, watching those war-weary, but now hysterically happy people. They filled the streets and sidewalks and Green Park, celebrating in the blaze of light from street lamps and shop fronts of this city that for almost eight years had not been lighted at night, except by fires from air raids.

I couldn't join in the fun because of a deep sadness I felt when I remembered the many good friends I had lost who were not here to share the victory for which they had given their lives. And again, there was nostalgia for the excitement and comradeship of life on a Squadron.

But it was over… No more waiting in the cockpit at the end of the runway, engine idling, eyes on one's number one, alert for the flare signalling it was time to go. No more the roar, and sudden rush of acceleration that pushed me back in the seat as the throttle was eased wide open, or the "clunk" of the wheels as they retracted into the wheel wells, and then the almost silent smoothness as we became airborne. No more gliding in over the entrance to the flare path and slipping onto the runway in darkness at mission's end.

I missed it all; waking to the sound of aircraft engines roaring into life in the early morning dawn, the excitement when the flare signalling "scramble" arched up overhead, and the occasional surprise when startled skylarks rose vertically at my feet as I strolled across the airfield and I missed the laughter and lively conversations and the "hi-jinks" in the Mess.

It was almost over, but then there was still Japan. The dying didn't stop. I got word that my good friend of long standing, Flight Lieutenant Jimmie Young (who had often expressed his premonition that he would be killed while flying) had "bought it" the day before. On a ferry flight in a Mustang, he ran into cloud and flew into a mountain. His dad had died earlier and he was his mother's only child.

Back at H.Q. a few days later, there was a call on the Tannoy instructing me to report to the station Adjutant. When I arrived, he had on his desk a very formal-looking document, as well as an envelope with the Royal Crown insignia impressed in sealing wax. The document contained instructions that I was to be sworn as a "King's Messenger on his Majesty's Service" and flown to Prestwick, Scotland that same afternoon, and to report to the Station Commander for further orders. The Adjutant explained I had to carry a sidearm and the sealed envelope, which was placed in a briefcase along with a message to the CO at Prestwick. It was never to leave my possession.

I hadn't a clue about what was going on. I had heard of "King's Messengers" but had no idea who they were, how they were selected or what their duties were. As the title inferred, I assumed they delivered important dispatches or papers, such as this sealed envelope, for the King. The Adjutant seemed to be impressed, but he couldn't tell me my ultimate destination or how long I would be gone.

We stopped by my billets and while the driver waited, picked up a shaving kit, a clean shirt, and an empty gas mask case as a carryall. Then I was delivered to Hendon where a little Miles Magister and its pilot were waiting. I was beginning to feel very important.

Upon arrival at Prestwick, I was immediately ushered into the CO's office. He opened the briefcase and the message, nodded a few times, and then attached an order: "F/Lt Smith is to deliver this sealed envelope to the Commanding Officer, RCAF Dorval, Canada." Now, this was good news! Perhaps I would be able to call home when I got there.

This sealed envelope must contain information too important, too secret, or too complicated to be entrusted to scrambled telephone conversations or coded wireless – so I thought. With my Webley revolver in its holster and the chained briefcase by my side, anyone could see that I was a man on a very important mission. No one asked questions, and in the dining hall that evening, I sat alone. I slept with the briefcase and sidearm under my pillow.

Two days of this, and then at 2:00am, I was awakened by a batman, and instructed to report to Flights immediately. They were waiting for me. A huge, clapped out B 24, or "Liberator," squatted out on the tarmac, all four props turning, lights ablaze. I could see the British roundels indicating it was RAF. I climbed on board, was given a parachute, a boxed meal, and a thermos of hot tea, and shown to a mattress on the floor of the bomb-bay. There was little thermal or sound insulation, and the noise on takeoff was deafening.

We stopped at the Azores for refuelling and then flew on to Canada and Dorval, a total of twenty-one hours and twenty-five minutes flying time. Lying there on that mattress, it was impossible to sleep as I tried to make some sense out of the events of the past month: posted from No. 65 Squadron to Ferry Command, two ferry trips to Italy, posted to Transport Command, then designated "King's Messenger," and now on my way to Dorval, Canada, with an important dispatch in a brown envelope with a red wax seal bearing the impression of the royal crown. I finally gave up and thought about the phone call I was going to make, if possible.

The pilot, Flight Lieutenant Bob Wilson, sent one of the crew back to tell me we were landing in a few minutes and to be ready to disembark as soon as possible. They were to continue on to Detroit, where the worn out old "Lib" would be rebuilt or scrapped. We touched down and taxied up to the ramp and I jumped out. There was a van waiting, and we headed for the office of the RCAF Commanding Officer of Dorval. It was about 10:00a.m., I hadn't shaved, and was looking rather scruffy, but I knew this dispatch had to be delivered immediately.

I was shown into Headquarters. I saluted and told the Adjutant I was Flight Lieutenant Smith reporting as King's Messenger with a dispatch to be delivered in person to his CO. I said this in a normal tone of voice, but the others in the room must have heard, and all typing, and conversation ceased immediately. One could have heard a pin drop. I think they all must have thought the war in Japan was over, or Churchill had died.

The Adjutant showed me into the CO's office, I saluted, handed him the envelope, and waited to be dismissed. He broke the seal, opened it, studied it for a moment, and then looked up and smiled. "Flight Lieutenant, do you know what's in this dispatch?"

"Certainly not, Sir; that seal was unbroken."

"Would you like to know what it says?" he asked.

"If you think I should, Sir… Yes, Sir."

The CO went on, "You must have some friends in pretty high places. It reads: 'The officer bearing this dispatch, Flight Lieutenant P. F. Smith, 134347 is to proceed to the United States on three weeks' leave – at the termination of which he is to return to Dorval, Canada, for transportation back to the United Kingdom.'"

I must be dreaming. How could this be?!

48. Home on Leave

I had only a few pounds sterling in cash, but the CO very kindly had his Adjutant prepare warrants for travel by rail to New York and exchanged my personal check on the Bank of England for $200 U.S. I left that same afternoon.

To say that I was excited would be an understatement. A few hours ago, I had no idea I would see the US for another few years, if ever, and now here I was on the way home! Would I ever know how or why this had happened?

The Canadian National Railway accepted my travel documents for "first class," that included a sleeper with an upper berth. There weren't many on board, a few civilians and the rest U.S. service personnel. My well worn RAF battle dress stuck out like a sore thumb. I sat in the almost-vacant rear observation car, watching the beautiful forest of Canadian pines race by, and trying to count the pheasants that jumped up on the tracks as we passed until they became too numerous. They must have been looking for scraps from the diner.

After an excellent meal, served on white linen with sparkling silverware, I fell into my "upper" on clean, crisp linen sheets; the first in three years, and slept like a log until we reached the border. There, a very officious conductor, despite my travel orders, tried to throw me off the train because I didn't have a passport and was in foreign uniform speaking like an Englishman trying to imitate an American. We had a few sharp words until his superior, hearing the ruckus, interceded, examined my papers, and seemed to be satisfied. I crawled back into bed and slept through to New York.

~ A Virginian in Best Blue ~

I finally arrived at La Guardia airport and Eastern Airlines again, was wonderful. They took a look at my RAF identification card and my uniform, and immediately produced the required priority. I paid for my ticket and caught the next flight out, late that evening, scheduled to arrive at Richmond at 2:15 a.m. I had five dollars and some change in my pocket and no idea where my parents' house was.

I was told Father had heard of "Rothesay," but having lost sight in his remaining good eye, had never seen it. It had been for sale for many months when Mother drove him by one Sunday afternoon and described it and the view overlooking the James River. The decision to move was made then and there. All I knew was the address, 1214 Rothesay Circle.

My flight landed pretty much on time. There were taxies waiting, but I had a bit of trouble convincing one that I had a home address, but no idea where it was, and would have to pay after we found it. We wandered around Rothesay for a half hour or more before we found 1214. There were no lights on, but I could see the upstairs windows were open and the noise of the taxi on the gravel driveway should have awakened Mother, who had always been a light sleeper. I called, "Anybody home?" For a moment there was no answer and then I heard, "Jim, there's someone outside and it sounds like Parke!"

They were genuinely surprised. They hadn't heard from me for several months due to censors' restrictions, and had no idea where I was other than "somewhere in England." They both hurried down the stairs in nightdress, then back up again to get money to pay the cabbie. Katherine and William, our two old retainers who lived on the place, were awakened by all the noise and joined in. It must have been 4:00 a.m. when father suggested that we all have a drink. That was quickly taken care of, and several hours later, in a state of exhaustion, we all went to bed.

How strange it was to be in bed in a room of my own. I tossed and turned on a mattress so soft that I couldn't sleep and I ended up on the floor. Mother found me there at daybreak "dead to the world" and thought I had lost my mind.

49. A Fateful Meeting

My long-time friend and ex-roommate at College, William Preston, student athlete, star of the football and basketball teams and a killer with the ladies, had a sister, Alice. He had spoken of her often but we had never met. After all, she was eight years younger than me – a little girl of only seventeen.

If anything was happening among those of our age group who happened to be in town, it usually took place at the soda fountain at the Country Club of Virginia. I was walking from the parking lot to the Club, when a station wagon with 'Fairfield' printed on the door passed by, filled with youngsters and driven by a laughing, pretty, dark-haired girl. The word Fairfield rang a bell; I recalled it was the name of the Preston family home, so this must be his "little sister." I waved and she stopped and backed up. I introduced myself as Billy's friend and got the biggest, brightest smile I had ever seen. We talked for a moment, awkwardly, in front of the others and I don't remember what was said, but I couldn't take my eyes off her.

That same afternoon, her mom and dad, Dr and Mrs Robert Preston, were kind enough to invite Mother, Father and me for cocktails. I hadn't known them well before the war, but found them to be very charming and easy to talk to. There was a formal portrait of Alice on a desk in their drawing room. In it she wore a black dress and a string of pearls. I told myself there and then that if I were ever to marry, it would have to be her.

For the next several weeks I saw no other girl. We were together constantly, swimming, dining, dancing and just "hanging out" together. I'm sure we created quite a stir with our families and friends, although nothing was ever said.

When my leave was over and it was time to go, Mom and Dad were rather upset and insisted that I stay. They had already lost one son and were obviously concerned for my safety. They reasoned the war in Europe was over, I had already done my job, and the RAF could do nothing to make me return since I was an American citizen; but I couldn't quite see it their way.

Alice – 1945.

It was difficult for them to understand, but after all, the British had trusted me enough to send me on this leave, with no assurance of my return, and knowing the temptations I would face. They had given me a chance to fly when my country had turned me down, and they had accepted my word regarding my training without documents to back me up, and had given me a posting to No. 65 Squadron (a Mustang Squadron) as promised.

There was also the matter of the oath I had taken to their King and a thing called "loyalty." The family realized all this, but they felt they had to try anyway.

On the morning I was to leave I had a telephone call. In those days, girls didn't call boys except in an extreme emergency. It was Alice. She wanted to say goodbye and wish me a safe return. I was so taken aback I hardly knew what to say, but I never forgot the call.

BRITISH EMBASSY,

WASHINGTON 8, D. C.

18th December, 1945

Dear Mr. Smith,

I have had your telegram and can understand and fully sympathize with desire to have your son back in time Christmas. I am very much afraid that with the present congestion in transport this is not likely to be found possible and we are not able at this end to be very helpful.

I am, however, arranging for a telegram to be sent at once to the Air Ministry asking that your son's passage should be expedited.

Yours sincerely,

Halifax

Mr. J.A. Smith, Jr.,
Eastern Building Supply Company,
209-210 Exchange Building,
Richmond 19, Virginia.

50. Back to "Blighty"

The train ride back to Dorval was slow, but it gave me time to review what had happened so far, and what I was likely to face in the future. I had attained the rank of Flight Lieutenant (equivalent to Captain in the US Army) and while the pay couldn't compare with that of the USAF, it was certainly sufficient to sustain one in England. It occurred to me that I might reenlist for another four years and have the opportunity to fly the jets and the "twin" Mustangs the Squadrons were beginning to be equipped with; but then what? I didn't feel that I was interested in a permanent career with the RAF. It was too soon to try to reach a decision, but it was worth thinking about.

At Dorval, a RAF Coastal Command Short Sunderland, a large, four-engine flying boat, was waiting, empty except for a crew of five. I was welcomed aboard as though I was still a King's Messenger, assigned a bunk, and invited to visit the "Front Office" whenever I wished. I spent most of the time up front asking questions and being questioned about the life of a "Fighter Boy." It was a delightful trip of twenty-two hours in the air via Botwood, Reykjavik, and on to Scotland.

The takeoff at Reykjavik was interesting. I had thought they would anchor or tie up to a dock to run up and test the engines. Not so. We were far out in the water when the port outer was taken to full power, and tested as the monster slowly turned a quarter circle. Then the starboard outer got the same treatment, turning us back the ninety degrees. The same sequence was followed for the two inner engines, and when all the checks had been completed, we stood pretty much where we had started.

The water was calm, there wasn't a whisper of wind, and to get the boat-like hull up on its "step," a high speed air-sea rescue boat was sent zigzagging down the flight path. This created enough wave motion to break the surface tension, and allow it to come unstuck. It still took a long, long run before we were airborne. All very exciting, particularly when we cleared the shoreline trees by no more than fifty feet!

As we landed in the Firth of Clyde near Gourock and taxied along the shore with its beautiful green fields, sloping down to the water, I wondered about my next assignment. Hoping I might be sent back to No. 65 or Ferry Command, I headed to Whitehall in London determined, if at all possible, not to be posted back to Transport Command HQ.

It just wasn't to be. I was posted back to that bloody Bushey Park for six months of the most boring duty I had experienced with the RAF. As Mess Secretary, my duties now were few but complicated by having to keep accounts (Try multiplying 6, or any number, times pounds, shillings and pence) and an eye on the alcohol when the amount of rations changed almost daily due to the transient officers coming and going and the thieving that took place. I was in the position of being accused of flogging the stuff so I turned the lot over to the WAAF Flight Sergeant, Jean MacArthur, knowing they would be very hesitant to take her to task.

My last flight was the delivery of British Army Major Forsythe from Hendon to Carlisle, then to Kingston and return to Hendon. (Hendon is now the site of the Royal Air Force Museum.) We took-off in early morning darkness in a little Percival Proctor. It was so dark and with no torch I could hardly see, and had to have the ground crew start the thing for us. It turned into a lovely, snowy September day, crisp and cold. The ground was covered in white which didn't help my navigation, but the Major was quite content and unaware of my difficulty in finding Carlisle. When we arrived, he hopped out, congratulated me, and disappeared.

The landing on my return to Hendon was my last on British soil, my last with the Royal Air Force, and my last flight as a pilot, for the next twenty years.

51. Demobbed

Hostilities in the Pacific ceased in August 1945, after they dropped the atom bomb, and Japan surrendered.

"Release" was based on "first in, first out" unless one was able to prove the need for one's presence at home. Using the "First in first out" criteria, I calculated I would not be "demobbed" until June of 1947. Nevertheless, I got a signal on December 20th 1945, posting me to No. 104 PDC (Personnel Discharge Centre) in Southampton.

At the PDC, we were all lined up, non-commissioned airmen, Flying Officers, Flight Lieutenants, Squadron Leaders, etc., in a huge hangar with long wooden tables piled with clothing. We were given a pair of shoes (choice of black or brown,) two pairs of socks, three pairs of underpants, three under-vests, a pair of grey flannel bags (trousers), a Harris tweed jacket, a necktie, and a tweed cap. We were allowed, of course, to keep our uniforms. I received a travel voucher to Richmond via New York, and 200 pounds sterling in separation pay was deposited in my bank in England.

There wasn't anyone to say goodbye except Flight Sergeant MacArthur, who drove me to the boat. The rest of my friends were scattered all over the country. It wasn't a very emotional farewell. After all, she was still in the "ranks," and I was an officer, but she did kiss me on the cheek and make a pretty little speech, thanking me for my help with "their troubles." As I was climbing the gangplank still dressed in my blue uniform, mingling with the thousands of homeward bound GI's in brown, I turned to wave, but she was gone.

52. Home for Good

The voyage to New York, again on HMS *Queen Elizabeth*, which usually took three to four days, started on December 20th, so we had an outside chance of being home for Christmas. However, we ran into one of the nastiest storms the Captain, Commander Bissett said he had ever experienced. We were practically hove-to, making zero progress for two days and didn't make New York until December 26th.

There was a tugboat strike in effect when we finally arrived, and the skipper for the first time, docked the mammoth ship, unaided, to the cheers of those on board as well as on shore. The troops were wildly excited. They were throwing a lot of their military clothing overboard and some even went over the side themselves, but were rescued, and taken ashore by the Coast Guard.

The family had no idea that I was on the way home, and once more, it was a middle-of-the-night arrival by taxi with no American funds. The Christmas tree was lighted, and having missed four Christmases in a row, it was indeed a welcome sight. The "cabbie" accepted an invitation for a drink, was paid, and drove off singing.

Alice's debut took place on the twenty-eighth and I was lucky enough to be able to take her home. Her escort was too "ossified" to drive, so I requested the privilege. It was hard to tell who was the most excited that evening, she or I, but I think I know – lucky me!

I had never had the slightest touch of "homesickness" while away. But here at home, years later, on occasions, I still have a longing for England, and those years with the RAF – strong enough to almost cause a visceral hurt, and a deep depression – a depression that will probably continue to recur until the day I "fall off the perch." Yet, I am one of the lucky ones. When I think of all those wonderful lads who didn't make it, the question always remains, "Why me?"

~ END ~

Sometimes on sleepless nights my mind wanders back to the mystery of that three week leave. I'll never know for sure, but I would be willing to wager it was the work of that kindly AOC who promised to send me to a Mustang Squadron when I, at his request, gave up my leave in order to instruct at Hawarden. He had the rank and privilege to make it happen.

If he was the one responsible, "God bless him!"

AIR MINISTRY,

ADASTRAL HOUSE,

KINGSWAY, W.C.2.

30th June, 1946.

Sir,

Upon the occasion of your resigning your commission, I am commanded by the Air Council to convey to you their thanks for the services which you have rendered to the Royal Air Force during a period of grave national emergency.

I am, Sir,

Your obedient Servant,

Flight Lieutenant P.F. Smith,
Royal Air Force Volunteer Reserve.

G.107391.

My letter of thanks from the Air Ministry.

By the KING'S Order the name of
Flight Lieutenant P.F.Smith
Royal Air Force,
was placed on record on
14 June, 1945,
as mentioned in a Despatch for distinguished service.
I am charged to express
His Majesty's high appreciation.

Harold Macmillan

Secretary of State for Air

It was nine years later, 1955, when I received a very official-looking envelope in the mail addressed to "F/Lt P. F. Smith." It contained a parchment with the insignia of the Royal Crown, embossed in gold.

The Author's Wartime Flying Statistics

Flying hours

Squadron	Sorties	Hours
No. 253	30	40:50
No. 225	88	109:45
No. 65	11	35:00
Total Operational	129	185:45
Non-Operational		2,353
Total flying hours		2,538:45

Aircraft flown

Military	Civil
Harvard Mk II	Cap 10
Hawker Hurricane Mk I	Cessna 150
Hawker Hurricane Mk II	Cessna 410
Hawker Hurricane Mk IIc	Decathlon
Miles Magister	Eagle Rock
Miles Master Mk II	Falco
Miles Master Mk I	Messerschmidt 209
Mustang Mk III	Piper Cub J 3
Mustang Mk IV	Pitts S2
Mustang P51 Mk I	Pitts Special
North American AT 6	Ryan STA
Purcival Proctor	Stearman
Ryan PT19	Taylorcraft
Spitfire Mk IX	Waco RNF
Spitfire Mk Vb	
Spitfire Mk Vc	
Spitfire Mk VIII	
Stearman	
Vultee BT 13	

May 8th 1945

Now there is nothing, not even our rank,
To witness what we have been;
And I am returned to my job in the bank,
And you to your margarine.

With apologies to Kipling